Advances in Game-Based Learning

Series Editors
Dirk Ifenthaler
Scott Joseph Warren
Deniz Eseryel

More information about this series at http://www.springer.com/series/13094

Sangkyun Kim • Kibong Song • Barbara Lockee
John Burton

Gamification in Learning and Education

Enjoy Learning Like Gaming

Springer

Sangkyun Kim
Department of System & Management Engineering
Kangwon National University
Chuncheon-si, Kangwon-do
Korea (Republic of)

Kibong Song
The Center for Instructional Technology Solutions in Industry and Education (CITSIE)
Virginia Tech
Blacksburg, Virginia, USA

Barbara Lockee
School of Education
Virginia Tech
Blacksburg, Virginia, USA

John Burton
School of Education
Virginia Tech
Blacksburg, Virginia, USA

Advances in Game-Based Learning
ISBN 978-3-319-47282-9 ISBN 978-3-319-47283-6 (eBook)
DOI 10.1007/978-3-319-47283-6

Library of Congress Control Number: 2017950555

Printed on acid-free paper

This Springer imprint is published by Springer Nature
The registered company is Springer International Publishing AG
The registered company address is: Gewerbestrasse 11, 6330 Cham, Switzerland

Preface

In the current landscape of learning and performance, the use of educational games and gamification instructional strategies has received significant attention as a means of engaging learners across age groups, cultures, and contexts. Though game-based instruction is not a new concept, the more recent proliferation of recreational video games and ubiquitous adoption of personal computing technologies have accelerated the exploration and application of such games for educational purposes.

Enjoying Learning Like Gaming provides a comprehensive look at the rationale behind using games for learning, as well as detailed guidance on the features and processes of effective educational game design. The book begins by exploring the psychological and behavioral aspects of gamification, with a focus on concepts related to learner engagement and fun, along with some of the potential negative states associated with the use of games, such as addiction. The connection to learning and performance is also detailed, offering evidence regarding the potential for positive outcomes associated with the use of gamification strategies.

The book also includes an overview of what defines a game, exploring the evolution of how games have been defined and a variety of considerations in such definitions. Common features include goals, rules, and interactions. A wide array of different kinds of games have developed over the years; therefore, a classification of game types is also provided, describing the defining characteristics and purposes of each category.

The concept of "gamification" itself is examined in light of its role in education and learning. It is also helpful to understand how this approach is fundamentally connected to various kinds of economic systems, including the industrial economy, experience economy, and the related role of behavioral economics in the use of games for education and learning. Specifically, we examine theoretical propositions that underpin the use of games for learning, such as dual processing, anchoring, conformity, and punishment. The effects of using gamification are also discussed in terms of improvements in learning and behavioral change.

Awareness of the various learning theories associated with educational game design is helpful when planning game-based learning environments and in decision making related to specific gamification strategies. The theoretical features and research related to self-determination, achievement goal theory, social learning theory, and situated learning can help guide understanding of student engagement and behavior within educational games. The role of feedback and its effectiveness in learning and performance is also critical in planning learner interactions and outcomes within game-based learning programs. Knowing how and when to integrate feedback into the activities can impact the effectiveness of learning outcomes and learner engagement.

Learners have different perceptions of gamified learning activities, which in turn drives learner behaviors within such contexts. A variety of psychological states can be experienced within game play, necessitating our understanding of possible reactions and responses within such learning environments. Feelings of control, competition, discovery, fellowship, and relaxation are only a few of the many conditions in which learners may perceive when engaged in games for learning. Awareness of these conditions, along with guidance on how to elicit (or avoid) them through design strategies, is key to effective planning for gamified learning experiences. It is also important to consider how to manage challenging player behavior within such programs as well, posed by "griefers" and rule breakers.

Development of educational games can be assisted through awareness of different gamification frameworks and their elements. Gamification platforms are also plentiful, so a checklist for evaluating which may be most appropriate is provided. So many tools and systems are available for supporting the creation of innovative and effective game-based learning programs. Descriptions of different development apps and software systems are included, as well as detailed guidance on strategies for the instructional design process related to the creation of effective game-based experiences for learners.

While research has supported the positive outcomes related to the use of games for learning, there are also some legal and ethical issues that must be considered before choosing to integrate such systems into classroom use. The acquisition of personal data for analytics can result in some privacy issues, for example. Other challenges can relate to copyright and ownership when utilizing existing materials for game production. These kinds of issues can often be avoided through sensitivity about their implications before the use of games in the classroom.

Examining how others have employed educational games can offer models for adoption within our own contexts. A variety of cases are provided from educational settings, including STEM education with virtual laboratory environments for biology, chemistry, and general science explorations. Other exemplars include computer coding environments, mathematics, and disaster relief, as well as integrated programs that teach various math concepts alongside human body systems, genetics, and evolution. Cases in the liberal arts and social sciences include language learning, politics and government, economics, and leadership programs. These examples reflect both self-directed and collaborative kinds of approaches with mechanisms for self-assessment and also teacher monitoring. Exploring these stories of gamified learning utilization will hopefully inspire the reader's own unique and creative implementation strategies!

But, how does one get started with gamification in the classroom? There is no better way to understand the benefits and challenges of game-based learning than by becoming a player yourself. We close with guidance on how to initiate your own learning experiences so that you are well-prepared to plan effective and engaging gamified programs for your own learners. We wish you good luck and good gaming!

Chuncheon-si, Kangwon-do, Republic of Korea
Blacksburg, VA, USA

Sangkyun Kim
Kibong Song
Barbara Lockee
John Burton

Contents

About the Authors

Sangkyun Kim is a professor of systems and management engineering at Kangwon National University. He has served the Game Literacy Division of the Korea Game Society as a chairman and representative of the Education Gamification Forum. He has earned the Teaching Excellence Award three times from Kangwon National University. He received his Ph.D. in cognitive science and a master's degree in industrial engineering from Yonsei University, Seoul, South Korea, and a bachelor's degree in control and instrumentation engineering from Chung-Ang University, Seoul, South Korea.

Kibong Song is an adjunct faculty at Virginia Tech. He has worked as a learning solution expert in corporates and higher education institutions. He has published books and articles on learning environment, talent development, and e-learning evaluation method. He earned his Ph.D. in curriculum and instruction with a concentration in instructional design and technology from Virginia Tech; a master's degree in industrial engineering from Yonsei University, Seoul, South Korea; and a bachelor's degree in computer science and engineering from Dongguk University, Seoul, South Korea.

Barbara Lockee is a professor of instructional design and technology at Virginia Tech. She has served as a president for the Association for Educational Communication and Technology and a director of the Office of Educational Research and Outreach. She has published more than 80 journal articles, conference proceedings, and books. She earned her Ph.D. in curriculum and instruction with a concentration in instructional technology from Virginia Tech and a master's degree in curriculum and instruction with a concentration in educational media and a bachelor's degree in communications media from Appalachian State University.

John Burton is a professor emeritus of instructional design and technology at Virginia Tech. Since 1977, he had served Virginia Tech as a professor, department chair, and director of the Center for Instructional Technology Solutions in Industry and Education (CITSIE). He has also contributed to the field by authoring more than

85 refereed articles, books, and instructional software. He received his Ph.D. in educational psychology from the University of Nebraska at Lincoln, a master's degree in experimental psychology from Illinois State University, and a bachelor's degree in psychology from the University of North Carolina at Chapel Hill.

Chapter 1
Beginning of Journey

Quest
Let's explore a simple example of gamification.
Let's figure out why we need gamification in learning and education.

1.1 Complete Your Mission

Many educators have been interested in motivating their students and helping them to engage in their learning. There are various approaches to student motivation. Gamification is one of them. This book describes some simple approaches for educators to gamify learning and instruction in the classroom. Your mission, as a reader of this book, is to ultimately be able to demonstrate your understanding of the concepts described in each chapter by applying the skills necessary to gamify instruction in your classroom. Sometimes learning by doing is more effective than just reading or listening alone. Before reading through the rest of this book, let's first design a simple game for motivating our students.

1.1.1 Background

Let's assume that you have two daughters. They both have something in common; neither of them is interested in learning math or using the self-teaching math books that you bought in order to enhance their math interest. They consider the books "boring" and do not want to read them. Another thing they have in common is that they both want to own princess dolls. In your efforts to find a solution that can help to motivate them to finally read their books, you discover gamification and believe that it may be the answer you've been looking for. You decide to develop a program

S. Kim et al., *Gamification in Learning and Education*, Advances in Game-Based Learning, DOI 10.1007/978-3-319-47283-6_1

using gamification that can motivate your daughters to read their textbooks. You name the program, "Saving the Princess."

1.1.2 Rules of the Game

The "Saving the Princess" program requires a game board, math books, virtual currency, and store that accepts the virtual currency. On the game board, there is a path made up of circles containing numbers (see Fig.1.1). These numbers represent the number of math questions (from the math books) that the players (your daughters) will need to answer before moving to the next circle. The players move forward on the game board, one circle at a time, after solving the requisite number of practice questions from their math books. The quantity of questions to be answered is determined by the number inside the circle. A player's game level goes up, and the number of practice questions to answer goes down, once they hit a lottery space. Finally, when players arrive at the castle space, they have completed the game requirements, and you have to buy the princess dolls for your daughters!

There are other incentives built into the game. Players receive virtual currency at each move (see Fig. 1.2). They can use the money only at the store accepting virtual currency. This "store" can be run by a parent or one of your friends. The store should be stocked with snacks, sweets, stickers, and small toys for the players to buy with their virtual money throughout the game.

At each lottery space, your daughters may pick one of the cards shown in Fig. 1.3. You must join in the activity on the drawn card with your daughters. For example, if they pick the kite-flying card, you have to help your daughters make and fly kites. If they choose the bonus 100 VC card, they can receive 100 VC in virtual currency.

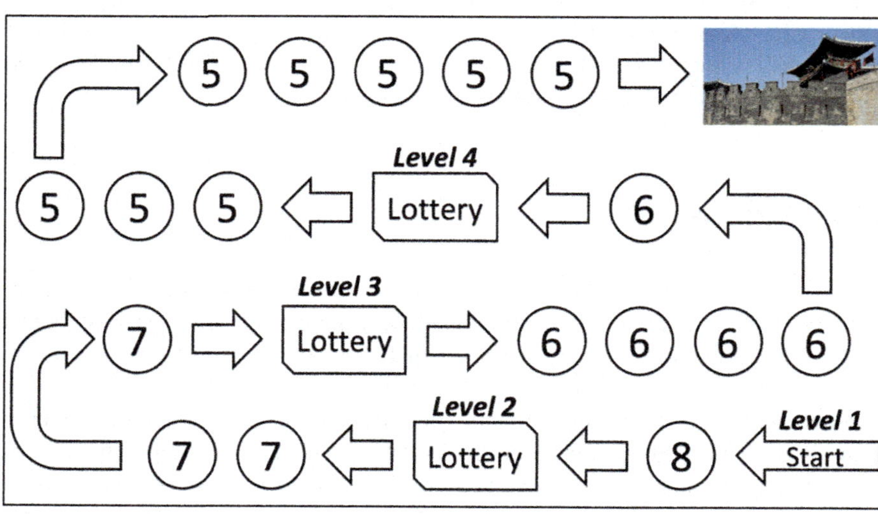

Fig. 1.1 Game board of "Saving the Princess"

Fig. 1.2 Virtual currency of the quest: Saving the Princess

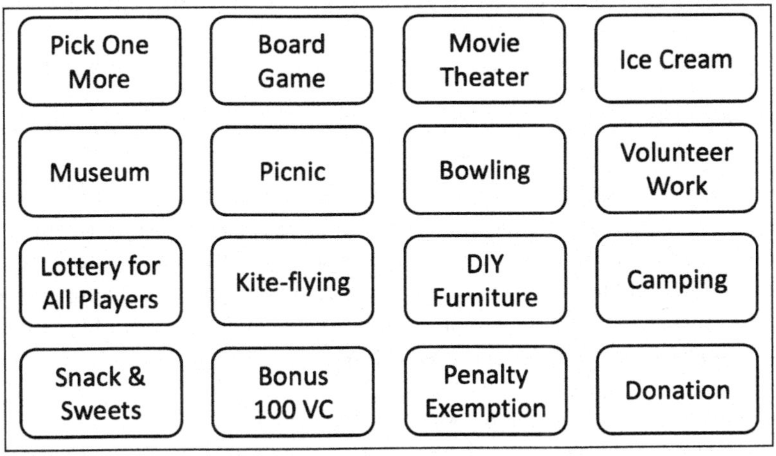

Fig. 1.3 Lottery of the "Saving the Princess"

The activities listed on the lottery card can vary depending on the outside conditions and your daughters' preferences. The most important rule here is to keep the game rules, including doing the activity, on the lottery cards.

1.1.3 Analysis of the Game

The number in each circle on the game board gradually decreases throughout the game. The number of circles in between lotteries increases as players move forward. In games, points, levels, and mechanics are frequently used. For example, if the sum of a player's game points reaches a specific number, the game level goes up. The player can increase the number of game points more easily at higher levels than lower ones. However, it is harder to achieve the next level at higher levels than lower ones. Players perceive a quick increase in game points, in the beginning stages of the game, as an increase in skills or abilities. Similarly, when a player takes a long time to build points and level up, in the later stages of the game, players perceive the value of each level as higher than before. "Saving the Princess" follows these game mechanics.

The virtual currency is an effective means of reward since the players can exchange the virtual currency with items that have real value. The player can be motivated by the increasing amount of virtual currency they receive as they move through the game, as well as their chances to purchase real items.

There are two kinds of reward systems in the game. One is virtual currency, which is a fixed reward system. The other is a lottery which is a variable reward system based on luck. While game players can anticipate the type and amount of rewards in the fixed reward system (by completing a specified task), they cannot in the variable reward system.

There is a card called "Lottery for All Players" among the lottery cards in this game. If a player picks this card, all the players have the benefits of the card. This is Karma, one of the game mechanics. The player who picked this card can be happy with doing a favor for other players.

1.1.4 Responses

You may observe unexpected responses from the players despite your best efforts. While some players can be motivated and deeply engaged in the game, some players aren't motivated and psychologically reject participation in the game. You should conduct pilot tests with some students from your group to find opportunities to improve this game and collect more positive results. One or more of the following player responses can result from playing "Saving the Princess."

- The players exhibit positive responses to the game.
- The players are motivated to solve the practice math questions from the textbook.
- The players have interest in other players' progress and achievements.
- The players give the princess doll (or other designated reward) a higher value, and then it would have had, had they not played the game.

1.2 Reasons Why We Need Gamification in Learning and Education

There will be a variety of people reading this book, to include lecturers at higher educational institutions, students majoring in education, teachers at K-12 schools, and professionals in talent development teams. No matter who the readers are, we surmise that all the readers have a common interest in making learning and education more enjoyable and fun.

Gamification is not just designed for learner fun and enjoyment. It is also an instructional approach that can be used to enhance the effectiveness of instruction on student learning. The readers of this book can expect that with gamification they will be able to:

- Increase student engagement and motivation.
- Enhance learning performance and academic achievement.
- Improve recall and retention.
- Provide instant feedback on students' progress and activity.
- Catalyze behavioral changes.
- Allow students to check their progress.
- Promote collaboration skills.

Your students can ultimately achieve their learning goals as a result of gamifying your instruction, in addition to making their learning more fun. The next chapter will discuss student engagement and fun. In Chap. 2, you will see how gamification, engagement, and educational effects are associated with each other.

Chapter 2
Engagement and Fun

Quest
Let's explore engagement and flow theory.
Let's find out how games use engagement and flow theory.
Let's figure out what the symptoms of over-engagement or addiction are.
Let's explore what alief is.

2.1 Engagement

Engagement is not a new concept to education. Many educators have been interested and concerned with student engagement for a long time. Engagement is "the heightened simultaneous experience of concentration, interest, and enjoyment in the task at hand" (Shernoff, 2013, p. 12) and the level of affective, behavioral, and cognitive involvement during a task (Connell & Wellborn, 1991).

Finn and Zimmer (2012) classified engagement types and defined each of them (see Table 2.1).

Student engagement is an important factor that affects academic success (Newmann, 1992), student motivation (National Research Council and the Institute of Medicine [NRC and IoM], 2004; Shernoff & Hoogstra, 2001), emotional and social learning outcomes (Klem & Connell, 2004), and academic performance (Nystrand & Gamoran, 1991; Shernoff & Hoogstra, 2001; Skinner & Pitzer, 2012).

2.1.1 Engagement and Flow Theory

According to Shernoff, Csikszentmihalyi, Schneider, and Shernoff (2003), the level of student engagement is high when the students' skills and the perceived challenge of a given task are in balance and the task is challenging. The researchers also suggest that

S. Kim et al., *Gamification in Learning and Education*, Advances in Game-Based Learning, DOI 10.1007/978-3-319-47283-6_2

Table 2.1 Finn and Zimmer's definition of engagement (2012)

Engagement	Definition
Academic engagement	"Observable behaviors related directly to the learning process" (p. 104)
Affective engagement	"Emotional response characterized by feelings of involvement in school as a place and a set of activities worth pursuing" (p. 104)
Cognitive engagement	"The expenditure of thoughtful energy needed to comprehend complex ideas in order to go beyond the minimal requirements" (p. 104)
Social engagement	"The extent to which a student follows written and unwritten classroom rules of behavior" (p. 104)

the learning environment should be under the students' control and the learning task should be relevant. This study is based on flow theory.

In flow theory, there are four mental states: anxiety, apathy, boredom, and flow (Csikszentmihalyi, 1975). Among them, flow is the optimal state for learning as it influences learning and academic achievement. Csikszentmihalyi (1990) defines flow as a mental state of complete absorption in an activity that is challenging but enjoyable.

The concept of flow theory is similar to Vygotsky's theory of zone of proximal development and Piaget's theory of cognitive development in that both theories support the idea that the effects of learning can be maximized when students engage in learning tasks that require the highest level of their abilities.

Csikszentmihalyi (2004) argues that individuals will engage in an activity when the activity is sufficiently challenging and performable. If the activity is too challenging, compared to an individual's skill, the individual tends to feel anxious and sometimes gives up trying to perform the activity. On the other hand, if the activity is too easy, the individual may feel bored and not want to perform the activity. Figure 2.1 illustrates the flow theory. In education, when students are in an anxiety zone, the teacher should improve students' skills or decrease the challenge level. On the contrary, when students are in a boredom zone, it can be better to give the students another activity that is more challenging.

When an individual is said to be experiencing flow, he or she engages in an activity, applies full concentration on the activity, becomes unaware of the passage of time, does not feel self-conscious, and appears to forget the surrounding environment (Perttula, Kiili, Lindstedt, & Tuomi, 2017).

Csikszentmihalyi (1997) suggested eight components of flow:

- Challenges match skills
- Clear goal
- Concentration and focus
- Control
- Direct feedback
- Loss of self-consciousness
- The activity becomes autotelic
- Transformation of time

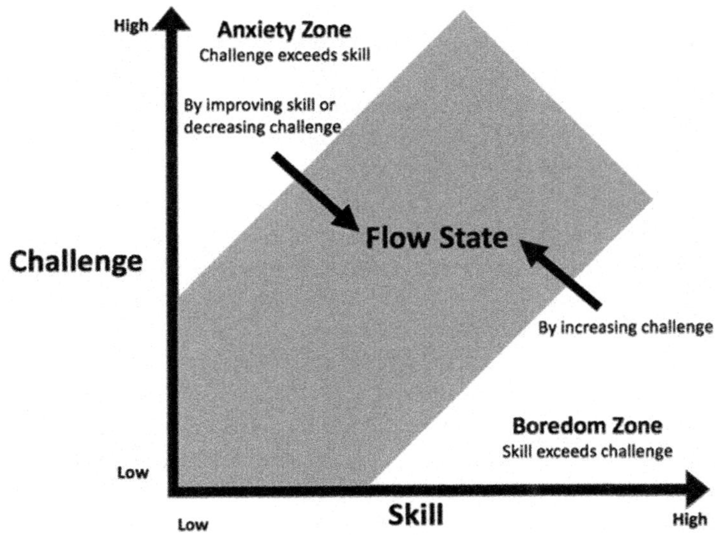

Fig. 2.1 Csikszentmihalyi's flow theory

From Csikszentmihalyi' idea, educators can consider some of the conditions of the learning environment that can help students engage in learning activities. The conditions may include clear goals, direct feedback, balance of challenge and skill, and learner control of the activity. Also, as a result of students' engagement, the teacher can observe concentration and focus, loss of self-consciousness, perception of distorted time passage, and dissipation of anxiety from his or her students.

2.1.2 Engagement in Games

Using flow theory, Radoff (2011) describes eight mental states that the game player can experience while playing a game: flow, arousal, control, relaxation, anxiety, worry, apathy, and boredom. Radoff (2011) posits that the player's mental states are subjectively determined by the player, based on the perceived challenge level of the game and the perceived skill of the player. Radoff's (2011) eight mental states are:

- Flow: Flow is the optimal mental state in which there is a balance between the challenge of the game and the player's skill. However, it is hard to keep flow state for the whole play time. Many games usually allow players experience arousal, control, and relaxation states during the play time.
- Arousal: In arousal state, the level of challenge in a game is somewhat higher than the player's skill level, but the gap can be closed by practices. If, however, this arousal state continues, the player tends to feel anxious and tired.
- Control: The player becomes proficient in the game and can control the situations within the game. The player can have satisfaction of playing the game when

the player can control the situations. If, however, the controllable situations last too long, the player loses interest in the game and feels bored.

- Relaxation: The player can seize perfect control of the situations within the game. If the period of relaxation continues to excess, the player may stop to play the game since the player feels bored. Relaxation can be considered to give the player a rest after highly challenging missions.
- Anxiety: The player perceives the challenge level is much higher than the skill level and makes a judgment that the player cannot successfully complete the game mission. The player with anxiety tries to find a solution shared by other players or adjust the level of difficulty. Some players give up the game since they feel despair and become lethargic.
- Worry: The player thinks the challenge level is moderate compared to the skill level, but the player cannot complete the game mission even after repeated practice. If the player continues to fail, the player perceives the mission as unachievable.
- Apathy: Both challenge and skill levels are very low. There are few chances to practice the skills since the missions in the game are too easy and simple to conduct. Apathy can be the opposite concept of flow.
- Boredom: The player has some level of skill, but the challenge level is too low. After attaining certain level of skills, the player wants to improve the skill by conducting more challenging missions.

According to Radoff (2011), while the player has a tendency to abandon the game when the player feels anxiety, worry, apathy, and boredom, the player is more likely to have positive experiences from playing the game when the player feels flow, arousal, control, and relaxation.

2.2 Fun

Fun is "a social emotional interactive process which deconstructs the social and historical biographical inequalities of lived experience to create a with-equal other social-human bond" (Podilchak, 1991, p.134). Fun is a subset of enjoyment (Strean & Holt, 2000) and an emotional state that can be experienced regardless of goals and rewards (Podilchak, 1985).

There are still arguments about the difference between fun and enjoyment. People sometimes use these terms interchangeably. Also, most English dictionaries do not separate these two terms. However, fun is somewhat different than enjoyment. Fun is a positive emotional or psychological state that an individual can have during or after a spontaneous and enjoyable activity. On the other hand, enjoyment is the activity itself, irrespective of the emotional or psychological change as its result.

In our daily lives, there are various activities that can create fun. Some of the activities are goal-oriented, but many are not. Some activities involve more than one person, but others can be carried out by one person. Figure 2.2 illustrates a framework to see different types of the activities that can create fun.

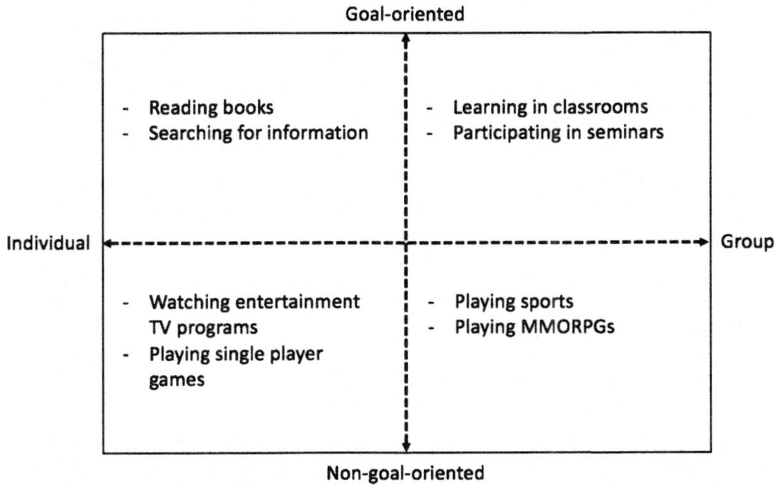

Fig. 2.2 Classification of activities creating fun

- Non-goal-oriented individual activity
- Non-goal-oriented individual activities do not have a clear goal and can be carried out by an individual. These types of activities include watching entertainment television programs, reading magazines, and playing games for single player. These activities commonly embed storytelling. People are able to conduct these types of activities even when they are psychologically or physically tired. However, the extent of fun created by these type activities is relatively weak and does not last long.
- Non-goal-oriented group activity
- Non-goal-oriented group activities do not have a clear goal and can be conducted by more than one person. These types of activities include playing sports and massive multiplayer online role playing games (MMORPGs). Interaction between people in the group is important to create fun. The higher level of interaction the activity has, the deeper engagement people are able to experience.
- Goal-oriented individual activity
- Goal-oriented individual activities have a clear goal and can be carried out by an individual. These types of activities include reading books on a specific topic, making something to solve a problem, and searching for necessary information. It is not easy to continue these types of activities until achieving the goal since there are few means to provide feedback on the activity and progress.
- Goal-oriented group activity
- Goal-oriented group activities have a clear goal and can be conducted by more than one person. These types of activities include learning in classrooms, communicating with other people for a common goal in online forums, and participating in seminars. Goal-oriented group activities are based on a common goal, feedback, and implicit and explicit consensus on activity principles. Thus, these types of activities are more likely to help participants engage in the activity than other types of activities.

The activities, creating fun, provide various experiences for the participants. Korhonen, Montola, and Arrasvunori (2009) suggested the Playful User Experience (PLEX) model to classify the playful experiences. The researchers included 20 categories for the PLEX model: captivation, challenge, competition, completion, control, discovery, eroticism, exploration, expression, fantasy, fellowship, nurture, relaxation, sadism, sensation, simulation, subversion, suffering, sympathy, and thrill. The details of each of the categories will be discussed more in Chap. 7.

2.3 Over-engagement or Addiction

There are still arguments on which term is more appropriate to indicate the negative situation in which the player excessively enjoys playing games. Some insist that *addiction* should be used rather than *over-engagement* since the positive images of engagement can cosmeticize (made to appear better than) a game addiction. On the contrary, some support using *over-engagement* instead of *addiction* as they consider the effects of using *addiction* on game industry and try to separate game addiction from drug addiction and alcohol addiction.

Young (2009) argues that it is important to know the warning signs or symptoms of game addiction or over-engagement. The researcher includes the following behaviors as warning signs or symptoms:

- Playing the game is the top priority
- Lying about playing the game
- Losing interest in other activities or hobbies
- Becoming less social and spending more time alone
- Preferring friends within the game to existing friends or family
- Becoming defensive about the need for the game
- Getting angry when deprived chances to play the game
- Feeling loss and becoming anxious or depressed when without the game
- Considering the game as a psychological escape
- Continuing to play the game in spite of the results negatively influencing real life

In addition to the above symptoms, the following are also considered symptoms of game addiction:

- Having eating disorders
- Having low self-esteem
- Having hostile behaviors and aggression toward family and friends
- Feeling confused
- Playing the game longer and longer over time
- Becoming apathetic toward future life and goals
- Becoming neurotic
- Losing self-control
- Having trouble sleeping
- Spending excessive money for the game

Playing games can provide people with various playful experiences, but game addictions can have a negative effect on their lives. They must be careful of how they use the game. The game should not be the top priority of their life. It should exist for enhancing the life.

2.4 Alief

Games utilize fictional and virtual worlds. Due to this fact, some people are easily distracted from the situations within the game while playing the game. To solve this problem, game designers should look into the concept of alief though some researchers are skeptical about its existence. The understanding of alief can offer an idea on a useful means to help players to concentrate on the game. People sometimes make a decision based on their beliefs created by conscious intention rather than objective evidence. Though they know that the beliefs are far from the truth, they intentionally rely on these beliefs.

Gendler (2008a) tried to explain this kind of phenomenon and suggested a definition of alief:

> An alief is a mental state with associatively-linked content that is representational, affective and behavioral, and that is activated – consciously or non-consciously – by features of the subject's internal or ambient environment. Aliefs may be either occurrent or dispositional (p. 642).

Aliefs are arational, associative, automatic, affect-laden, action-generating, conceptually antecedent to other cognitive attitudes that the creature may go on to develop, and are shared by human and non-human animals (Gendler, 2008b).

In applying alief for designing a game, it is more important to make quality scenarios and game mechanics than visual graphics or sound effects. Game designers should consider when and how the player can experience alief. Players can experience alief in the beginning of the game or regularly. Some games use operant conditioning to form alief.

References

Connell, J. P., & Wellborn, J. G. (1991). Competence, autonomy, and relatedness: A motivational analysis of self-esteem processes. In M. R. Gunnar & L. A. Sroufe (Eds.), *Self-processes in development: Minnesota symposium on child psychology* (Vol. 23, pp. 167–216). Hillsdale, NJ: Erlbaum.

Csikszentmihalyi, M. (1975). *Beyond boredom and anxiety*. San Francisco, CA: Josey-Bass.

Csikszentmihalyi, M. (1990). *Flow: The psychology of optimal experience*. New York, NY: Harper Perennial.

Csikszentmihalyi, M. (1997). *Finding flow: The psychology of engagement with everyday life*. New York, NY: Basic Books.

Csikszentmihalyi, M. (2004). *Good business: Leadership, flow, and the making of meaning*. New York, NY: Viking.

Finn, J. D., & Zimmer, K. S. (2012). Student engagement: What is it? Why does it matter? In *Handbook of research on student engagement* (pp. 97–131). Boston, MA: Springer. doi:10.1007/978-1-4614-2018-7_5

Gendler, T. S. (2008a). Alief and belief. *The Journal of Philosophy*, *105*(10), 634–663.

Gendler, T. S. (2008b). Alief in action (and reaction). *Mind & Language*, *23*(5), 552–585.

Klem, A. M., & Connell, J. P. (2004). Relationships matter: Linking teacher support to student engagement and achievement. *Journal of School Health*, *74*(7), 262–273.

Korhonen, H., Montola, M., & Arrasvunori, J. (2009). Understanding playful user experience through digital games. In A. Guenand (Ed.), *Proceedings of the 4th International Conference on Designing Pleasurable Products and Interfaces, DPPI 2009* (pp. 274–285). Compiègne, France: ACM Press.

National Research Council and the Institute of Medicine [NRC and IoM]. (2004). *Engaging schools: Fostering high school students' motivation to learn.* Washington, DC: The National Academies Press.

Newmann, F. M. (1992). *Student engagement and achievement in American secondary schools.* New York, NY: Teachers College Press.

Nystrand, M., & Gamoran, A. (1991). Instructional discourse, student engagement, and literature achievement. *Research in the Teaching of English*, *25*(3), 261–290.

Perttula, A., Kiili, K., Lindstedt, A., & Tuomi, P. (2017). Flow experience in game based learning–a systematic literature review. *International Journal of Serious Games*, *4*(1). doi:10.17083/ijsg.v4i1.151

Podilchak, W. (1985). The social organization of "fun". *Loisir et Société/Society and Leisure*, *8*(2), 685–691.

Podilchak, W. (1991). Distinctions of fun, enjoyment and leisure. *Leisure Studies*, *10*(2), 133–148.

Radoff, J. (2011). *Game on: Energize your business with social media games.* Indianapolis, IN: Wiley Publishing.

Shernoff, D. J. (2013). *Optimal learning environments to promote student engagement.* New York, NY: Springer.

Shernoff, D. J., & Hoogstra, L. (2001). Continuing motivation beyond the high school classroom. *New Directions in Child and Adolescent Development*, *93*, 73–87.

Shernoff, D. J., Csikszentmihalyi, M., Schneider, B., & Shernoff, E. S. (2003). Student engagement in high school classrooms from the perspective of flow theory. *School Psychology Quarterly*, *18*(2), 158–176. doi:10.1521/scpq.18.2.158.21860

Skinner, E., & Pitzer, J. (2012). Developmental dynamics of student engagement, coping, and everyday resilience. In S. L. Christenson, A. L. Reschly, & C. Wylie (Eds.), *Handbook of research on student engagement* (pp. 21–44). New York, NY: Springer.

Strean, W. B., & Holt, N. L. (2000). Coaches', athletes', and parents' perceptions of fun in youth sports: Assumptions about learning and implications for practice. *Avante*, *6*(3), 83–98.

Young, K. (2009). Understanding online gaming addiction and treatment issues for adolescents. *The American Journal of Family Therapy*, *37*(5), 355–372.

Chapter 3
What Is a Game?

Quest

Let's understand the definition of games.
Let's find out the characteristics of games.
Let's figure out what kinds of games exist and how to classify them.

3.1 Definition and Characteristics of Games

One of the most famous definitions of what a game is comes from game designer and producer, Sid Meier, which states, "a game is a series of interesting and meaningful choices made by the player in pursuit of a clear and compelling goal." Many researchers agree with this definition (Barwick, Dearnley, & Muir, 2011; Falstein, 2005; Juul, 2004; Kim & Lee, 2015; McGinnis, Bustard, Black, & Charles, 2008; Sullivan, Mateas, & Wardrip-Fruin, 2012).

Prior to Meier's definition, game was commonly defined as "an activity directed toward bringing about a specific state of affairs, using only means permitted by specific rules, where the means permitted by the rules are more limited in scope than they would be in the absence of the rules, and where the sole reason for accepting such limitation is to make possible such activity" (Suits, 1967, p. 156).

Game has been also defined as "a rule-based play with determined goals" (Groh, 2012, p. 39), "a set of activities involving one or more players" (Dempsey, Haynes, Lucassen, & Casey, 2002, p. 159), or "a system in which players engage in an artificial conflict, defined by rules, that results in a quantifiable outcome" (Salen & Zimmerman, 2004, p. 80).

However, there are some issues with the existing definitions of game. Let's think about the following questions.

- Is a game always interesting to everyone?
- Isn't there a single activity that can be a game?

S. Kim et al., *Gamification in Learning and Education*, Advances in Game-Based Learning, DOI 10.1007/978-3-319-47283-6_3

A game can be uninteresting to some. People occasionally join in a game for their social relationships irrespective of their interest. Thus, interest is not a necessary element for defining a game. Also, some games consist of a simple rule and a single activity. For example, players throw a ball as far as they can to decide a winner. Their activity can be a game all in itself. Thus, a game is always a set of activities.

Some researchers (Crookall, Oxford, & Saunders, 1987; Garris, Ahlers, & Driskell, 2002; Leemkuil, de Jong, & Ootes, 2000; McGonigal, 2011; Schell, 2008) have studied the characteristics of games. Crookall et al. (1987) argued that the characteristics of games include goals, strategies, rules, competition and cooperation, and chances. Garris et al. (2002) classify the characteristics of games into fantasy, rules/goals, sensory stimuli, challenge, mystery, and control. McGonigal (2011) includes goals, rules, feedback systems, and voluntary participation as characteristics of games. Leemkuil et al. (2000) described four essential characteristics of games. Games:

- Have goals that must be reached
- Include constraints, rules, and incentives
- Have competition
- Are situated in a specific context

Schell (2008) more specifically listed the characteristics of games. Games:

- Are entered willfully
- Have goals
- Have conflict
- Have rules
- Have win and lose
- Are interactive
- Have challenge
- Create their own internal value
- Engage players
- Are closed formal systems

A review of the above-listed studies shows the common characteristics of games to be goals, rules, and interactions. Goals are a player's desired outcomes from playing a game. While some goals can be achieved by only one player, some others allow multiple players to achieve. This difference is a factor influencing players' interaction.

Rules are promises or agreements for playing a game. With the rules, players know what they need to do and what can occur within a game. Rules are usually defined before beginning a game, but some rules can be modified, created, or removed in accordance with the players' agreement.

Interactions are reciprocal actions between a player and another player, a player and a game, a group of players and another group of players, and a group of players and a game. The interactions within a game include competition, conflict, challenge, feedback, control, perception of an event, feelings, and results of a game (Rogers, 2017).

In the context of this book, the following definition of "game" will be used:

> A game is an action or a set of actions, that includes one or more people, objects, or animals, usually in competition with others, that follow a specific set of rules, in order to achieve a goal.

3.2 Types of Games

There are various views on game types. Some of the views (Eilon, 1963; Juul, 2005; Murray, 1952) are focused toward a specific game type while others focus on all games in general. For example, focusing on specific game types, Murray (1952) classified board games into alignment or configuration games, hunt games, mancala games, race games, and war games. Juul (2005) suggested a typology for classifying video games. The researcher argued that there are just five video game types: abstract, iconic, incoherent world, coherent world, and staged games. Eilon (1963) classified business games based on two criteria: design characteristics and purpose. Apperley (2006) included action, adventure, simulation, role playing, and strategy in video game types.

Some researchers focusing on all game types, in general, include Aarseth, Smedstad, and Sunnanå (2003), Elverdam and Aarseth (2007), and Vossen (2004). Vossen (2004) discussed three classification distinctions that can be used when classifying games: competitive/noncompetitive, interactive/noninteractive, and physical/nonphysical. Based on the classification distinctions, the researcher classified games into noncompetitive-nonphysical games, parallel-nonphysical games, interactive-nonphysical games, noncompetitive sports, parallel sports, and interactive sports.

Aarseth et al. (2003) suggested a multi-dimensional typology of games to classify the type of game based on spatial movement. The researchers suggested five meta-categories and 13 dimensions. The five meta-categories include space, time, player-structure, control, and rules. The 13 dimensions include perspective, topography, environment, pace, representation, teleology, player-structure, mutability, solvability, determinism, topological rules, time-based rules, and objective-based rules. Based on this typology, Elverdam and Aarseth (2007) suggested a modified typology consisting of *eight* meta-categories and *17* dimensions. The eight categories include virtual space, physical space, external time, internal time, player composition, player relation, struggle, and game state. The 17 dimensions include virtual perspective, virtual positioning, environment dynamics, physical perspective, physical positioning, representation, teleology, haste, synchronicity, interval control, composition, stability, evaluation, challenge, goals, mutability, and solvability (see Table 3.1).

Theoretical perspectives of game classification systems have been discussed so far. For a better understanding of the practical application of game type classification, Table 3.2 shows how companies like Apple and Google classify games on their online stores.

The action game genre is a game type that requires physical movement of a game character or a player. In an action game, players need to quickly react to dynamic situations. For example, they need to detect enemies as soon as possible and take appropriate action with an optimal solution, to their given situation. Shooting games and fighting games are representative subgenres of the action game. Examples are ARMA 3, Batman, Bulletstorm, Call of Duty, Counter-Strike, Deer Hunter, Dishonored, Doom, Gears of War, Grand Theft Auto, Saints Row, SWAT 4, and Wolfenstein, which fall into the action game type.

Table 3.1 Elverdam and Aarseth's (2007) typology

Meta-categories	Dimensions	Values
Virtual space	Perspective	Omnipresent, vagrant
	Positioning	Absolute, relative
	Environment dynamics	None, fixed, free
Physical space	Perspective	Omnipresent, vagrant
	Positioning	Location based, proximity based, both
External time	Representation	Mimetic, arbitrary
	Teleology	Finite, infinite
Internal time	Perspective	Present, absent
	Synchronicity	Present, absent
	Interval control	Present, absent
Player composition	Composition	Single player, two players, single team, two teams, multi-players, multi-teams
Player relation	Bond	Dynamic, static
	Evaluation	Individual, team, both
Struggle	Challenge	Predefined, instanced, adversary
	Goals	Explicit, implicit
Game state	Mutability	Temporal, finite, infinite
	Solvability	None, conditional, unlimited

Table 3.2 Game categories of Apple App Store and Google Play

Apple App Store	Google Play
Action	Action
Adventure	Adventure
Arcade	Arcade
Board	Board
Card	Card
Casino	Casino
Dice	Casual
Educational	Educational
Family	Music
Music	Puzzle
Puzzle	Racing
Racing	Role playing
Role playing	Simulation
Simulation	Sports
Sports	Strategy
Strategy	Trivia
Trivia	Word
Word	

The adventure game genre is a game type in which the player explores and solves problems within a narrative content. Most adventure games are driven by a narrative. An adventure game can be useful to improve problem-solving skills (Oblinger, 2006). The adventure genre has been more focused by educational researchers than the other game types (Ju & Wagner, 1997; Quinn, 1994). Examples are Gemini Rue,

Indiana Jones and the Fate of Atlantis, King's Quest, Last Window: The Secret of Cape West, The Longest Journey, and To The Moon, which all fall into the adventure game type.

The action game and adventure game genres sometimes form a blended genre together. The action-adventure genre is a game type that includes the characteristics of both action and adventure genres. Examples of some of the most popular action-adventure games are Assassin's Creed, Batman: Arkham Knight, BioShock, Legend of Zelda, Metal Gear Solid, and Resident Evil.

The arcade game genre is somewhat beyond the game types classified by content since it is a game type that can be run on a coin or card-operated machine installed in amusement arcades, bars, or other businesses. As game consoles for homes have been popular, the arcade game business entered a state of decline. However, arcade games have been developed for various devices, such as smartphones, tablets, game consoles for homes, and computers. Games such as Donkey Kong, Galaxian, Pac-Man, Space Invaders, and Street Fighter were popular in the era of arcade games. Angry Birds, Asphalt, Fruit Ninja, Impossible Twisty Dots, and Worms are currently popular arcade game types.

The board game genre is technically all kinds of games that can be played on a board. In a board game, the player places pieces on specific positions of the board according to the game rules. 7 Wonders Duel, Acquire, Checkers, Chess, Clue, Discworld, Dominion, Go, Monopoly, Mysterium, Risk, Scrabble, and Star Realms are some of the most famous board games.

The card game genre is a game type that uses a deck of cards as the primary game means. A card game usually consists of players, game cards, a game board, and a set of rules. Due to its design simplicity and flexibility, card games have been used in diverse areas including education. Some researchers (Baker, Navarro, & Van Der Hoek, 2005; Mariscal, Martinez, & Marquez, 2012; Rastegarpour & Marashi, 2012) have found the effects of using card games on learning. Card games can also be useful for enhancing pattern recognition and concept matching (Oblinger, 2006). Apples to Apples, Canasta, Contract Bridge, Crazy Eights, Magic: The Gathering, Play Or Pay, Poker, Slapjack, Taboo, and Uno are examples of card games.

The casino game genre is a game type in which gamblers can play to pursue financial gains, often in a casino. Like the arcade game genre, the casino game genre is beyond the game types classified by content. A casino game includes different kinds of games, such as card games and board games. Also, a casino game is not limited to a specific physical space, such as a casino, any longer. A casino game can be played any place and time, including on the internet. Baccarat, Blackjack, Craps, Keno, Poker, Roulette, Slots, and Solitaire are some of the most popular casino games.

The educational game genre is a game type that was made to support learners in their efforts to acquire knowledge, skills, and attitudes on a topic or field (Dell'Aquila et al., 2017). It focuses more on the educational purposes rather than entertainment. An educational game can be technically any type of game, as long as it meets the educational purposes. Crazy Machines: The Wacky Contraptions Game, Math Doodles, Monster Physics, Montessori Crosswords, Rocket Math, Stack the Countries, and Stack the States are examples of educational games.

The music game genre is a game type that uses the elements of music as the primary device for the game. Within a music game, the gamer plays musical instruments, sings songs, dances to music, or composes music. Beaterator, Beat Gather, Dance Dance Revolution, DefJam Rapstar, DJ Hero, Guitar Hero, Patapon, Rock Band, Rocksmith, and SingStar are examples of games belonging to this game type.

The puzzle game genre is a game type in which the player fits pieces of various shapes and colors together to complete the target image. Since the emergence of smartphones and tablets, new interaction methods, like swiping a screen by a finger, have been added to the typical means for playing these types of games. Because of the new interaction methods and new technologies, puzzle games have become more various and aesthetic. Within a puzzle game, the player uses intuition, pattern recognition, logical thinking skills, problem-solving skills, and memory to solve puzzles. Because of this, puzzle games are sometimes used for educational purposes. Agar.io, Candy Crush, Dots, Lemmings, Portal, Puzzle Craft, Scribblenauts, and Tetris are examples of the most popular puzzle game types.

The racing game genre is one of the oldest game types. It is a game type in which the player controls a game character to win a racing competition by running, driving a vehicle, or other types of movements. The player, in some racing games, needs to complete additional missions during the race. The additional missions may include collecting game items, removing obstacles, and upgrading the vehicle. Using game consoles for the home, such as Playstation, Wii, and Xbox, players can be required to run, jump, or physically move in some other way, to complete a race. Assetto Corsa, Dirt, Driver, F1, Forza Horizon, Mario Cart, iRacing, Project CARS, Shift, Test Drive, TrackMania, and Trials Fusion are examples of this type of racing game.

The role-playing game genre (RPG) is a game type that requires the player to take on the role of a game character with specific missions and quests in a fictional setting. In some RPGs players organize themselves into teams in order to achieve a common goal. The players develop their own individual game character and game items, such as weapons, resources, and bases. With communication capabilities provided by the internet, the players are able to share the game tasks necessary to complete a mission. There are also subgenres of RPGs, such as action RPGs (ARPG), massively multiplayer online RPGs (MMORPG), tactical RPGs (TRPG), and turn-based RPGs. Dungeons & Dragons, Final Fantasy, The Witcher, Mass Effect, Fallout, and Diablo belong to the role-playing game type.

The simulation game genre is a game type that simulates a real world or a fictional situation. The player in the simulation game experiences situations that they cannot or would not normally experience in a real-world setting. Some simulation games have non-entertainment goals, such as training and research (Kim & Watson, 2017). Quinn (1994) claims that simulation games have been a focal point for educational researchers more than the other game types. ARMA, DCS World, Euro Truck Simulator, Falcon, Farming Simulator, Flight Simulator X, Football Manager, Kerbal Space Program, OMSI, Silent Hunter, Style Boutique, The Sims, Train Simulator, Transport Tycoon are examples of some of the most popular simulation games. Business games are sometimes considered separate from simulation games. The purpose of a business genre game type is training, strategy testing, or research for businesses. In a business game, the player tries to find the optimal solution and make decisions for achieving business goals and objectives. AdVenture Capitalist, Anno, Brass, Capitalism, Gazillionaire, GoVentureWorld, Hipster CEO, Industry Giant, Informatist, INNOV8, Marty Raygun's Fistful of Dollars, OpenTTD, SimCEO, The EIS Simulation, The Patrician, Platform Wars, Tropico, and Steam: Rails to Riches are examples of the business game type.

The sports game genre is a game type in which the player competes with other players or game characters in a sport or recreational setting using the same sets of rules, equipment, space, and referees as that of non-game sports. With the advancement of technologies that gamers can use, the sports genre has been implemented in various manners. For example, with new human-computer interface devices, such as augmented reality, motion detection, virtual reality, and wearable devices, the sports genre has become more authentic and immersive than before. Archery Master 3D, Fishing Hook, FIFA, WWE, Football Manager, Madden NFL, MLB Perfect Inning, NBA Live, NHL, Pro Evolution Soccer, Rocket League, and WGT Golf Game are examples of the sports game type.

The strategy game genre is a game type in which the player tries to achieve the goals and objectives by planning, executing, and reflecting on strategies and tactics within the game's story. Strategy games are usually based on scenarios. During the game, the player strategically uses available resources and the character's ability to complete a mission or quest designed in a game scenario. Cities: Skylines, Civilization, Crusader Kings II, Endless Legend, Offworld Trading Company, StarCraft, Total War: Shogun 2, Warcraft, and XCOM 2 are examples of the strategy game genre. The subgenres of the strategy game include 4X (eXplore, eXpand, eXploit, and eXterminate), real-time strategy, tower defense, turn-base strategy, and wargames.

The trivia game genre is a game type in which the player solves quizzes that can be interesting but insignificant in various subjects. Players can easily participate in this type of game due to the simplicity of the rules. As a result, this game has been used for family gathering and social meetings. Some corporations use this type of game for team building and change management. In education, the trivia game has been used for promoting conceptual knowledge and communication. Brain Quest Smart Game, Dibs, Jeopardy, Matter of Fact, MoviePop, Outburst, QuizUp, Scene It?, Smarty Party, TriviaBurst, Trivia Crack, Trivia Pursuit, Wits & Wagers are examples of some of the most popular trivia games.

The word game genre is a game type in which the player, using a given set of rules, discovers or creates a word or a phrase, or guesses a word or a phrase from a hint. In education, some teachers use word games for reinforcing students' memory for what they have learned. 7 Little Words, Crossword Light, Heads Up, Letterpress, Word Brain, Word Search Epic, Wordament, and Words With Friends are examples of the word game type.

The game types discussed in this chapter do not represent a complete listing and depending upon the perspective on the game and its traits, other game types could be added to the list. Also, the emergence of new technologies and the convergence of existing game types make the classification more complicated or even impossible. It is hard to define a unified framework for classifying game types, but understanding the game types and their characteristics can help educators to generate ideas for gamifying their instructions.

References

Aarseth, E., Smedstad, S. M., & Sunnanå, L. (2003). A multi-dimensional typology of games. In M. Copier & J. Raessens (Eds.), *Proceedings of Level Up Conference* (pp. 48–53). Utrecht, Netherlands: Utrecht University & Digital Games Research Association.

Apperley, T. H. (2006). Genre and game studies: Toward a critical approach to video game genres. *Simulation Gaming, 37*(1), 6–23.

Baker, A., Navarro, E. O., & Van Der Hoek, A. (2005). An experimental card game for teaching software engineering processes. *Journal of Systems and Software, 75*(1), 3–16.

Barwick, J., Dearnley, J., & Muir, A. (2011). Playing games with cultural heritage: A comparative case study analysis of the current status of digital game preservation. *Games and Culture, 6*(4), 373–390.

Crookall, D., Oxford, R. L., & Saunders, D. (1987). Towards a reconceptualization of simulation: From representation to reality. *Simulation/Games for Learning, 17*(4), 147–171.

Dell'Aquila, E., Marocco, D., Ponticorvo, M., di Ferdinando, A., Schembri, M., & Miglino, O. (2017). Learn to lead: An educational game for leaders to be. In *Educational games for soft-skills training in digital environments* (pp. 123–140). Cham, Switzerland: Springer International Publishing.

Dempsey, J. V., Haynes, L. L., Lucassen, B. A., & Casey, M. S. (2002). Forty simple computer games and what they could mean to educators. *Simulation & Gaming, 33*(2), 157–168.

Eilon, S. (1963). Management Games. *Operational Research, 14*(2), 137–149.

Elverdam, C., & Aarseth, E. (2007). Game classification and game design: Construction through critical analysis. *Games and Culture, 2*(1), 3–22. doi:10.1177/1555412006286892

Falstein, N. (2005). Understanding fun: The theory of natural funativity. In *Introduction to game development* (pp. 71–98). Boston, MA: Charles River Media.

Garris, R., Ahlers, R., & Driskell, J. E. (2002). Games, motivation, and learning: A research and practice model. *Simulation & Gaming, 33*(4), 441–467. doi:10.1177/1046878102238607

Groh, F. (2012). Gamification: State of the art definition and utilization. In *Proceedings of the 4th seminar on Research Trends in Media Informatics* (pp. 39–46). Ulm, Germany: Institute of Media Informatics Ulm University.

Ju, E., & Wagner, C. (1997). Personal computer adventure games: Their structure, principles, and applicability for training. *ACM SIGMIS Database, 28*(2), 78–92.

Juul, J. (2004). Introduction to game time/time to play: An examination of game temporality. In N. Wardrip-Fruin & P. Harrigan (Eds.), *First person: New media as story, performance and game* (pp. 131–142). Cambridge, MA: MIT Press.

Juul, J. (2005). *Half-real: Video games between real rules and fictional worlds*. Cambridge, MA: MIT Press.

Kim, J. B., & Watson, E. (2017, January). Exploring practical potentials of business simulation games. In *Proceedings of the 50th Hawaii International Conference on System Sciences* (pp. 725–734). Waikoloa, HI.

Kim, J. T., & Lee, W. H. (2015). Dynamical model for gamification of learning (DMGL). *Multimedia Tools and Applications, 74*(19), 8483–8493.

Leemkuil, H., de Jong, T., & Ootes, S. (2000). *Review of educational use of games and simulations*. EC project KITS (IST-1999-13078), KITS Deliverable D1, Enschede, The Netherlands: KITS consortium. Retrieved December 4, 2016, from http://doc.utwente.nl/28235/1/review_of_educational.pdf

Mariscal, A. J. F., Martinez, J. M. O., & Marquez, S. B. (2012). An educational card game for learning families of chemical elements. *Journal of Chemical Education, 89*(8), 1044.

McGinnis, T., Bustard, D. W., Black, M., & Charles, D. (2008). Enhancing e-learning engagement using design patterns from computer games. In *Proceedings of the First International Conference on Advances in Computer-Human Interaction* (pp. 124–130). Sainte Luce, Martinique: IEEE Computer Society Conference Publishing Services.

McGonigal, J. (2011). *Reality is broken: Why games make us better and how they can change the world*. New York, NY: Penguin Press.

Murray, H. J. R. (1952). *A history of board-games other than chess*. London, UK: Oxford University Press.

Oblinger, D. (2006). *Simulations, games, and learning*. ELI White Paper. Retrieved from http://mobilelearningcourse.pbworks.com/f/Games+and+Learning+ELI3004.pdf

Quinn, C. N. (1994). Designing educational computer games. In K. Beattie, C. McNaught, & S. Wills (Eds.), *Interactive multimedia in university education: Designing for change in teaching and learning* (pp. 45–57). Amsterdam, The Netherland: Elsevier.

Rastegarpour, H., & Marashi, P. (2012). The effect of card games and computer games on learning of chemistry concepts. *Procedia – Social and Behavioral Sciences, 31*, 597–601. doi:10.1016/j.sbspro.2011.12.111

Rogers, R. (2017). The motivational pull of video game feedback, rules, and social interaction: Another self-determination theory approach. *Computers in Human Behavior, 73*, 446–450.

Salen, K., & Zimmerman, E. (2004). *Rules of play: Game design fundamentals*. Cambridge, MA: MIT press.

Schell, J. (2008). *The art of game design: A book of lenses*. Burlington, MA: Morgan Kaufmann Publishers.

Suits, B. (1967). What is a game? *Philosophy of Science, 34*(2), 148–156. Retrieved from http://www.jstor.org.ezproxy.lib.vt.edu/stable/186102

Sullivan, A., Mateas, M., & Wardrip-Fruin, N. (2012). Making quests playable: Choices, CRPGs, and the grail framework. *Leonardo Electronic Almanac, 17*(2), 146–158.

Vossen, D. P. (2004). The nature and classification of games. *AVANTE-ONTARIO, 10*(1), 53–68.

Chapter 4
What is Gamification in Learning and Education?

Quest

Let's explore the types of games that can be applied for gamification.
Let's understand the definition of gamification.
Let's find out the historical background of gamification.
Let's figure out how gamification is associated with the experience economy and the behavioral economics.
Let's understand the effects of gamification on learning and education.

4.1 Games and Gamification

As we discussed in the previous chapter, there are many different types of games with which people engage. In this chapter, we discuss game types that are associated with educational gamification, as well as game type characteristics.

4.1.1 Types of Games for Gamification

Among the various game types that are closely related to gamification, there are war games, simulation games, serious games, and alternate reality games.

4.1.1.1 War Game

Although the war game type has been applied in other fields, such as business and education, the concept of war games has been developed for military purposes. A war game helps military organizations to evaluate the effects and results of military strategies and tactics. The war game can be conducted by software alone or in

S. Kim et al., *Gamification in Learning and Education*, Advances in Game-Based Learning, DOI 10.1007/978-3-319-47283-6_4

combination with military exercises. Through the use of scenarios, a war game can be used for testing the effectiveness and value of a plan, strategy, tactic, and resources in the course of war and battle preparation.

In education, especially in the disciplines like business administration, industrial engineering, and economics, the war game has been used for learning strategies and decision making. Likewise, many corporations have used war games for planning and evaluating business strategies.

Gilad (2008) suggested seven elements of the war game genre, which are as follows:

- Realistic
- Empowering
- Accessible
- Lots of fun
- Inexpensive
- Simple
- Transparent

4.1.1.2 Simulation Game

A simulation game type is a game genre that simulates real-world situations or virtual situations. There are many areas to use a simulation game. Among them, business administration is one of the most intriguing fields. The first modern business simulation game was developed by the RAND Corporation in 1955. It was named Monopologs. The US Air Force used Monopologs to improve the performance of their logistics system and inventory management (Faria, 1998; Faria & Wellington, 2004; Jackson, 1959).

Since the emergence of simulation games and the computer system, the usage of simulation games has been expanded to other fields. Since the early 1990s, some business functions, such as strategies, financial management, accounting, marketing, and sales, have all used the simulation game type for improving performance. Since the diffusion of the internet and the spread of information technologies, web-based simulation games have also been used for education. In addition, the simulation game type is not limited to a specific time and space anymore. With smartphones and tablet PCs, people can enjoy the simulation game now.

4.1.1.3 Serious Game

A serious game is a game that is developed for a purpose other than entertainment (Ulrich & Helms, 2017). It is also called an applied game. Zyda (2005) defined the serious game type as “a mental contest, played with a computer in accordance with specific rules that uses entertainment to further government or corporate training, education, health, public policy, and strategic communication objectives” (p. 26).

Djaouti, Alvarez, Jessel, & Rampnoux (2011) claimed that some games have been produced to support serious purposes. According to the researchers, The Oregon Trail game can be considered an ancestor of some the serious games in the education field. Don Rawitsch, Bill Heinemann, and Paul Dillenberger developed this game in 1971 and the Minnesota Educational Computing Consortium (MECC) produced this game in 1974 with the purpose of teaching students about American history during the middle nineteenth century.

4.1.1.4 Alternate Reality Game (ARG)

An alternate reality game is a game that requires involvement in the real world (McGonigal, 2011). Unlike most other game genres, the ARG employs real-world media to deliver its component. The delivery media include text messaging, email, social network service, and websites (Gilliam et al., 2017). Barlow (2006) argues that the ARG is a game in which gamers can play in both the real world and a virtual online world assuming that a virtual event happens in the real world. Being aware of some of the fundamental concepts related to ARGs, such as puppet masters, curtains and trailheads, will help to better understand the ARG (Dominik, 2008; Olbrish, 2011).

Puppet masters are people who design and operate the ARG. They help other gamers to play without revealing their status and roles. A curtain in an ARG is a device that hides the puppet masters and the fact that the puppet masters manage the story flow within the game. The main role of the curtain is to help gamers experience the natural story development while playing the game. A trailhead is a clue that provides information on the game. The trailhead can be exposed to potential gamers through social network services, websites, emails, or sometimes non-electronic media. The role of the trailhead is to help gamers be more involved in the game.

4.1.2 Definition of Gamification

Gamification is to change something that is not a game through a game or its elements (van Grove, 2011; Werbach & Hunter, 2012). Gamification can be a means to engage employees in tasks (Reeves & Read, 2009), promote collaboration (McGonigal, 2011), or improve motivation (Zichermann & Linder, 2013). Deterding, Dixon, Khaled, and Nacke (2011) suggested defining "gamification" as "the use of game design elements in non-game contexts" (p. 9). In this book, however, a somewhat specific definition is used to help readers understand the concept of gamification more clearly.

Gamification is
A set of activities and processes
To solve problems

By using or applying the characteristics of game elements

The above definition is quite important to understand the exact meaning of gamification for the following reasons:

- Gamification is not a single activity but a set of relevant activities and systematic processes.
- Gamification should have a purpose to solve specific problems.
- Merely using game mechanics, like badges and points, should not be considered gamification. Gamification should be based on the characteristics of game elements.

4.1.3 Historical Foundations of Gamification

In many cases, it is difficult to trace the precise origin of a concept. With this in mind, there are many ideas on the origin of gamification. It is possible that some could argue that reward systems in a kingdom from thousands of years ago could be an early version of gamification. As there are many possible variations to gamification's starting point, this section discusses some meaningful examples of gamification from the past that have led to current forms of gamification, rather than tackling gamification's entire timeline.

A meaningful step was made by Sperry & Hutchinson (S&H) in the use of gamification in America. The company began a stamp business in 1896. Grocery stores, gas stations, and other retailers distributed the S&H stamps to their customers based on the amount of money customers spent on their products. The customers could then exchange the collected stamps for products such as various housewares. The S&H stamp business can be an example of gamification, particularly with a purpose of improving customers' loyalty. In the 1980s, American Airlines (AA) provided another example of using gamification in business through its frequent flyer program, started in 1981. The purpose of this program was to encourage new customers and to retain old ones. Following AA's program, in 1983, Holiday Inn began a similar loyalty program to encourage travelers to stay in Holiday Inns across the USA.

For educational purposes, games such as The Oregon Trail and Lemonade Stand were produced in 1970s. In 1980s, more efforts to use gamification for education were made. The following are some of those efforts.

- MasterType (1981)
- Rocky's Boots (1982)
- Typo Attack (1982)
- Stickybear ABC (1984)
- Where in the World is Carmen Sandiego? (1985)
- Number Munchers (1986)
- Odell Lake (1986)
- Reader Rabbit (1986)

- Math Blaster (1987)
- Mavis Beacon Teaches (1987)
- SimCity (1989)

4.1.4 Definition of Gamification in Learning and Education

Gamification can be useful for learning and instruction because it can promote learner engagement. The fact that many educators face problems related to student interest and engagement in their classrooms is not new to education. In the past, educators have tried to use a variety of interventions, including the use of motivational strategies. However, the effect of the intervention lasted for only a short period of time. Due to its fun and playful nature, gamification can be a good solution to help solve learner engagement and participation issues in the classroom.

This book defines "gamification in learning and education" as follows:

Gamification in learning and education is
A set of activities and processes
To solve problems related to learning and education
By using or applying the game mechanics

To have a more clear understanding of the meaning of gamification in learning and education, it may be helpful to see the relationship between serious games and gamification in learning and education (see Fig. 4.1).

Serious games for learning and education are games that are developed for the purpose of achieving learning and education objectives in the real world. Game players can learn while they are playing the game and have achieved the objectives when

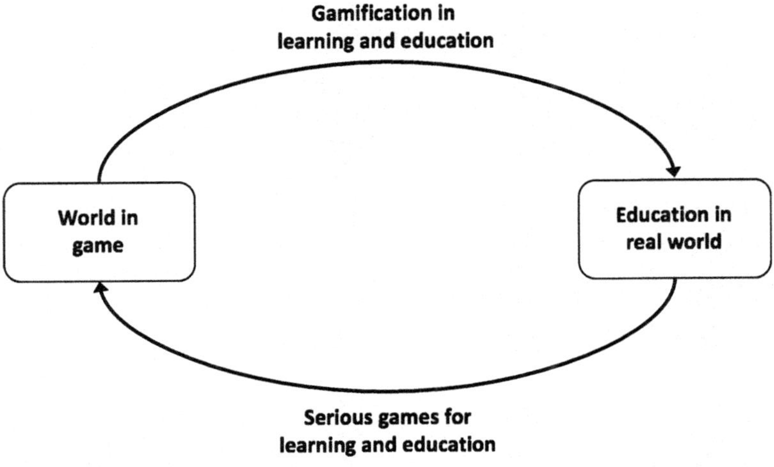

Fig. 4.1 Relationship between serious games for learning and education and gamification in learning and education

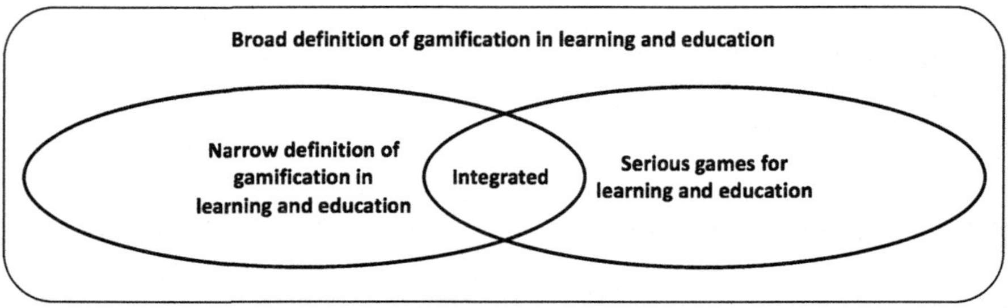

Fig. 4.2 Redefining the relationship between serious games and gamification in learning and education

they successfully complete the missions in the game. That is, the serious games, with real world problems, are implemented within games. On the other hand, the purpose of gamification in learning and education is to create real-world environments that support learning and problem solving. It is implemented within the real world.

Considering the definition of gamification in learning and education described previously, serious games should be included in gamification in learning and education because they are also a set of activities and processes to solve problems related to learning and education by using or applying the game mechanics. Thus, the relationship between serious games and gamification in learning and education should be redefined as shown in Fig. 4.2.

The broad definition of gamification in learning and education includes serious games for learning and education, narrow definition of gamification in learning and education, and the integrated game type at the intersection of these two concepts. This book uses the broad definition for describing gamification in learning and education.

4.2 Gamification and Economics

The relationship between gamification and economics is interactive. Gamification can be used for economic purposes, such as advertising a product, increasing customer loyalty, and engaging potential customers. Conversely, however, gamification uses economics and economics theories as fundamental mechanisms. This section discusses experience economy and the behavioral economics associated with gamification.

4.2.1 Gamification and Experience Economy

Pine and Gilmore (1998, 1999) suggested the concept of experience economy to explain a new source of value to which customers attach importance. They argue that experiences can be another economic offering in addition to commodities, goods, and services. According to the experience economy, experience in the past and future brings people happiness that cannot be explained by the existing three

Table 4.1 Economic distinctions

Economic offering	Experiences	Commodities	Goods	Services
Economy	Experience	Agrarian	Industrial	Service
Economic function	Stage	Extract	Make	Deliver
Nature of Offering	Memorable	Fungible	Tangible	Intangible
Key Attribute	Personal	Natural	Standardized	Customized
Method of supply	Revealed over a duration	Stored in bulk	Inventoried after production	Delivered on demand
Seller	Stager	Trader	Manufacturer	Provider
Buyer	Guest	Market	User	Client
Factors of demand	Sensations	Characteristics	Features	Benefits

Note: Adapted from "Welcome to the experience economy," Pine, B. J. and Gilmore, J. H., 1998, *Harvard Business Review*. Copyright 1998 by Harvard Business Publishing.

economic offerings. Pine and Gilmore (1998) also claimed that experiences are more differentiated and have more premium economic value than the other three values. Table 4.1 compares experience with the other three economic offerings.

As shown in Table 4.1, there are four economic offerings: commodities, goods, services, and experiences (Pine & Gilmore, 1998, 1999). Experience is a core value of the experience economy, and corporations try to engage customers in memorable events that can create planned experiences. In this type of scenario, corporations stage the experiences and customers are guests in the experience economy. Empirical studies (Nicolao, Irwin, & Goodman, 2009; Van Boven & Gilovich, 2003) support the experience economy. The researchers argue that positive purchase experiences tend to create more happiness than material purchases.

Based on the study by Van Boven and Gilovich (2003), Carter and Gilovich (2010) compared experiential purchases with material purchases. They found that people's satisfaction with material possessions tended to be weaker than those with experiences by comparing them to other options. They also found that people's satisfaction with material purchases decreased over time, but those with experiential purchases increased over time (see Fig. 4.3).

Now, let's discuss education. Publishing books and producing learning tools are part of an *industrial* economy. Teaching and supporting students are part of a *service* economy. Then, what can be the experience economy in the education field? This book suggests the use of gamification for the experience economy in education because of the following advantages of gamification:

- Active engagement: Students can find enjoyment and actively engage in their classes using the story, dynamics, and mechanics of games.
- Learning effect: Gamified learning and education can help students to remember what they learned more deeply and for a longer period of time.
- Personal experience: Students can create their own experiences by completing given missions and getting rewards, such as points, levels, or badges.

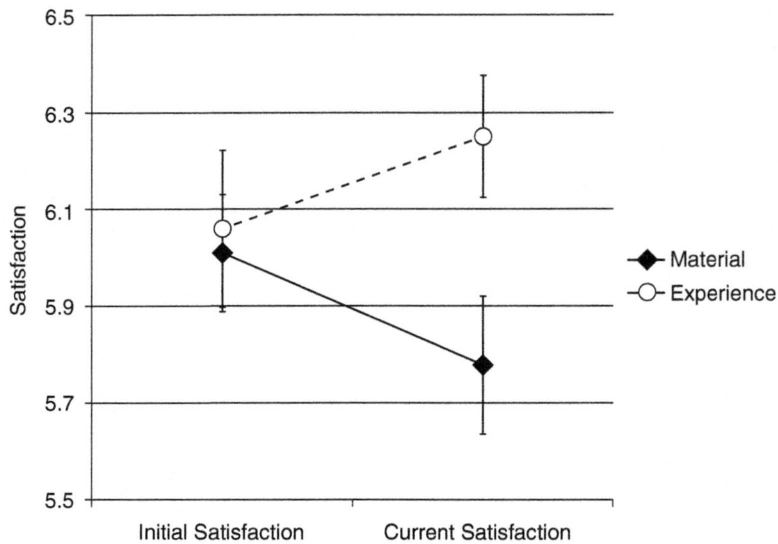

Fig. 4.3 Initial and current satisfaction with earlier material and experiential purchases (Reprinted from "The relative relativity of material and experiential purchases," by Carter and Gilovich (2010), Copyright 2010 by American Psychological Association)

There are many benefits of using gamification for learning and education in addition to the above. However, gamification cannot solve all the problems in learning and education. As people still use the old economic offerings, the solutions to solve the problems should include traditional or existing methods as well as gamification.

4.2.2 *Gamification and Behavioral Economics*

Behavioral economics is an economics field that explains economic decisions and phenomena from the perspectives of psychology, physiology, and sociology. Understanding behavioral economics can begin with the rejection of the ideas of complete rationality and unlimited cognition. In behavioral economics, individuals are sometimes fallible, irrational, and impatient and have limited cognitive ability.

This book discusses some behavioral economics topics that can be applied to gamifying learning and education.

4.2.2.1 Dual Process Theory

Dual process theory is based on parallelism, with the assumption that the mechanisms of information processing or mental process can be divided into two categories: heuristics and reasoning. These two categories have also been called as

"Automatic and Controlled" (Schneider & Shiffrin, 1977a, 1977b), "Unconscious and Conscious" (Wilson, 2002), "Type 1 process and Type 2 process" (Evans & Stanovich, 2013), and "System 1 and System 2" (Kahneman, 2011; Stanovich, 1999). This book uses System 1 and System 2 as the two mechanisms of information processing.

The System 1 and System 2 categories have different characteristics. While System 1 is automatic, intuitive, quick, easy, unconscious, experience-based, associative, implicit, and parallel, System 2 is analytical, controlled, slow, difficult, conscious, deliberative, reflective, rule-based, explicit, and serial.

When individuals use System 1 for making decisions, they do not need to use working memory, meaning that their decision will be determined by intuitive and automatics reactions. On the other hand, when they use System 2 for decision making, they use their working memory to process given information. For example, when a novice driver tries to parallel park or press a brake pedal, the driver usually tries to recall relevant prior knowledge. An experienced driver, however, reacts to similar situations automatically.

In games and gamified situations, players use System 1 to guess and estimate results when they have limited information and they face complicated situations. Players use System 2 to analyze and evaluate given information. From this conscious and systematic process, players can make decisions, such as planning strategies. The roles and characteristics of these two mechanisms can be used for gamification for learning and education.

4.2.2.2 Anchoring Effect

Anchoring effect is a phenomenon caused by a cognitive bias using an initial piece of information as a reference point in making decisions (Tversky & Kahneman, 1974). When an anchor is set, individuals' subsequent decision making can be influenced by the anchor since they use the anchor for evaluating the other information pieces. For example, customers interpret a discounted price of a computer as inexpensive and reasonably priced after looking at the discount percent and an original price marked on the price tag. Because of this kind of phenomena, many business fields use the anchoring effect.

Games also use the anchoring effect. Game players start a game from the easiest mission and conduct more difficult missions step by step. Because of the anchoring, players think subsequent missions are possible. For example, players at level 1 cannot figure out how to complete missions for level 5, but players at level 4 who successfully completed level 1, 2, and 3 can conduct missions at level 5. Gamification for learning and education can use the anchoring effect to relieve the perceived difficulty of a task that learners may have. Instead of suggesting a long-term, ultimate, and difficult goal in the beginning, teachers can use the anchoring for assigning learning tasks to learners. Learners who successfully complete a task can have increased self-efficacy perceptions and may be more likely to have confidence to move on to the next level task.

4.2.2.3 Conformity

Conformity is a conforming behavior caused by social pressure from a majority group. Individuals tend to conform to the opinion from a majority group regardless of their own opinions (Asch, 1952, 1955). This phenomenon occurs even when the opinion from the majority group is wrong or has a flaw (Thaler & Sunstein, 2008). The causes of conformity can include attitudes designed to maintain social norms (Milgram, 1992) and the adjustment of opinions through the considering of other opinions (Mackie, 1987). Factors affecting conformity include group size (Asch, 1952, 1955), culture (Bond & Smith, 1996), neural differences (Campbell-Meiklejohn, Bach, Roepstorff, Dolan, & Frith, 2010), and task importance and difficulty (Baron, Vandello, & Brunsman, 1996).

Gamification for learning and education can employ this conformity to improve learning performance. By sharing the information on other students' achievements and rewards, a teacher can motivate students to attempt a task. The teacher can consider using the mechanisms of the leaderboard, levels, badges, and points.

4.2.2.4 Punishment

An experiment in Israel was conducted to see the effects of punishment for the parents who pick their kids up from a day-care facility after the service time (Gneezy & Rustichini, 2000). In the experiment, the punishment was a fine. It was anticipated that the number of parents who arrived late to the day-care facility would be reduced. After the fine system was imposed, however, more parents came late because they perceived the fine as a part of the service price. This result aligns with Robert Baden-Powell's quote on punishment, "correcting bad habits cannot be done by forbidding or punishment" ("Boy Scouts of America," n.d.).

Some teachers use punishment for deterring or repressing inappropriate behaviors in a class. Penalty points or deducting points is frequently used in a class. However, instead of punishment, positive reinforcement can be used for inducing expected behaviors. For example, a teacher can give a badge to a student who behaves well.

4.3 Effects of Gamification

There are still disagreements over the effectiveness of gamification on learning and education. However, many researchers have investigated the effects of gamification for learning and education and found positive relationship between gamification and desired outcomes (Aldrich, 2005; Anderson & Rainie, 2012; Domínguez et al., 2013; Faria & Whiteley, 1990; Gee, 2003; Hakulinen, Auvinen, & Korhonen, 2013; Kumar & Khurana, 2012; Li, Grossman, & Fitzmaurice, 2012; Mayo, 2009; Michael & Chen, 2005; Nah, Zeng, Telaprolu, Ayyappa, & Eschenbrenner 2014; Prensky,

2001; Quinn, 2005; Randel, Morris, Wetzel, & Whitehill, 1992; Smith & Baker, 2011; Sitzmann, 2011; Su & Cheng, 2015). Among the various effect types, the discussion in this section focuses on learning achievement and psychological and behavioral changes.

4.3.1 *Learning Achievement*

Learning achievements can be one of the most important outcomes in learning and education. When educators consider the use of gamification, one of their considerations is whether or not it enhances students' learning achievement. Many researchers (Domínguez et al., 2013; Faria & Whiteley, 1990; Li et al., 2012; Mayo, 2009; Nah et al., 2014; Randel et al., 1992; Smith & Baker, 2011; Sitzmann, 2011; Su & Cheng, 2015) have revealed that gamification for learning and education can improve learning achievement.

Gamification can enhance higher order thinking skills (Domínguez et al., 2013), declarative knowledge and procedural knowledge (Sitzmann, 2011), and test performance (Faria & Whiteley, 1990; Li et al., 2012; Mayo, 2009; Nah et al., 2014; Randel et al., 1992; Smith & Baker, 2011; Su & Cheng, 2015; Yildirim, 2017).

The effects of gamification for learning and education vary depending on specific conditions, like the characteristics of content and audience. Mayo (2009) insists upon the relatively beneficial effect of gamified courses compared to traditional courses. The researcher analyzed the learning outcomes of gamified courses and traditional courses: algebra for high-school students, geography for college students, numerical methods for college students, ecology/biology for middle and high-school students, electrostatics for middle-school students, and cell biology for college students. The research showed that the students in gamified courses performed at least 7.2% better than the non-gamified courses. College students in a gamified cell biology class performed 40% better than the same lecture-based class. Also, Randel et al. (1992) argue that subject matters with specific content, like mathematics, can show higher positive effects of gamification than other subject matters.

4.3.2 *Psychological and Behavioral Changes*

The outcomes expected from learning include psychological and behavioral changes. Many educators experience difficulty in their classes because their students are not motivated and do not actively participate in class activities. Due to practical experiences such as this, motivation and engagement are the topics that educators and researchers have been interested in for a long time. Some researchers found the effectiveness of gamification on inducing psychological and behavioral changes. Hakulinen et al. (2013), Kumar and Khurana (2012), Li et al. (2012),

Nah et al. (2014), and Su and Cheng (2015) all claim that gamified learning can foster students' motivation and engagement. The psychological and behavioral changes resulting from gamification for learning and education are not limited to motivation and engagement. Sitzmann (2011) revealed that gamification promotes self-efficacy and increased retention.

References

Aldrich, C. (2005). *Learning by doing: A comprehensive guide to simulations, computer games, and pedagogy in e-learning and other educational experiences*. San Francisco, CA: Pfeiffer.

Anderson, J., & Rainie, L. (2012). Gamification and the internet: Experts expect game layers to expand in the future, with positive and negative results. *Games for Health Journal, 1*(4), 299.

Asch, S. E. (1952). Effects of group pressures upon the modification and distortion of judgments. In G. E. Swanson, T. M. Newcomb, & E. L. Hartley (Eds.), *Readings in social psychology* (2nd ed.). New York: Holt.

Asch, S. E. (1955). Opinions and social pressure. *Scientific American, 193*(5), 31–35.

Barlow, N. (2006). Types of ARG. In IGDA Alternate Reality Games SIG (Ed.), *2006 Alternate Reality Games White Paper* (pp.15-20). The International Game Developers Association. Retrieved from http://www.christydena.com/wp-content/uploads/2007/11/igda-alternaterealitygameswhitepaper-2006.pdf

Baron, R. S., Vandello, J. A., & Brunsman, B. (1996). The forgotten variable in conformity research: Impact of task importance on social influence. *Journal of Personality and Social Psychology, 71*(5), 915–927. doi:10.1037//0022-3514.71.5.915

Bond, R., & Smith, P. B. (1996). Culture and conformity: A meta-analysis of studies using Asch's (1952b, 1956) line judgment task. *Psychological Bulletin, 119*, 111–137.

Boy Scouts of America. (n.d.). *Pearls of wisdom-quotes from Baden-Powell*. Retrieved 10 September 2017, from http://www.scouting.org/filestore/pdf/Quotes.pdf

Campbell-Meiklejohn, D., Bach, D., Roepstorff, A., Dolan, R., & Frith, C. (2010). How the opinion of others affects our valuation of objects. *Current Biology, 20*(13), 1165–1170. doi:10.1016/j.cub.2010.04.055

Carter, T. J., & Gilovich, T. (2010). The relative relativity of material and experiential purchases. *Journal of Personality and Social Psychology, 98*(1), 146–159. doi:10.1037/a0017145

Deterding, S., Dixon, D., Khaled, R., & Nacke, L. (2011). From game design elements to gamefulness: Defining gamification. In *Proceedings of the 15th international academic MindTrek conference: Envisioning future media environments* (pp. 9–15). Tampere, Finland: ACM.

Djaouti, D., Alvarez, J., Jessel, J. P., & Rampnoux, O. (2011). Origins of serious games. In M. Ma, A. Oikonomou, & L. Jain (Eds.), *Serious games and edutainment applications* (pp. 25–43). London, England: Springer.

Domínguez, A., Saenz-de-Navarrete, J., de -Marcos, L., Fernández-Sanz, L., Pagés, C., & Martínez-Herráiz, J. J. (2013). Gamifying learning experiences: Practical implications and outcomes. *Computers & Education, 63*, 380–392.

Dominik, M. (2008). *The alternate reality game: Learning situated in the realities of the 21st century*. In Proceedings of EdMedia: World Conference on Educational Media and Technology (pp. 2358-2363). Vienna, Austria: Association for the Advancement of Computing in Education (AACE). Retrieved from https://www.learntechlib.org/p/28694/

Evans, J. S. B. T., & Stanovich, K. E. (2013). Dual-process theories of higher cognition: Advancing the debate. *Perspectives on Psychological Science, 8*(3), 223–241.

Faria, A. J. (1998). Business simulation games: Current usage levels-An update. *Simulation & Gaming, 29*(3), 295–308.

Faria, A. J., & Whiteley, T. R. (1990). An empirical evaluation of the pedagogical value of playing a simulation game in a principles of marketing course. *Developments in Business Simulation and Experiential Learning*, *17*, 53–57.

Faria, A. J., & Wellington, W. J. (2004). A survey of simulation game users, former-users, and never-users. *Simulation & Gaming*, *35*(2), 178–207.

Gee, J. P. (2003). *What video games have to teach us about learning and literacy*. New York: Palgrave Macmillan.

Gilad, B. (2008). *Business war games: How large, small, and new companies can vastly improve their strategies and outmaneuver the competition*. Pompton Plains, NJ: Career Press.

Gilliam, M., Jagoda, P., Fabiyi, C., Lyman, P., Wilson, C., Hill, B., & Bouris, A. (2017). Alternate reality games as an informal learning tool for generating STEM engagement among underrepresented youth: A qualitative evaluation of the source. *Journal of Science Education and Technology*, *26*(3), 295–308.

Gneezy, U., & Rustichini, A. (2000). A fine is a price. *The Journal of Legal Studies*, *29*(1), 1–17. doi:10.1086/468061

Hakulinen, L., Auvinen, T., & Korhonen, A. (2013). Empirical study on the effect of achievement badges in TRAKLA2 online learning environment. In *Proceedings of Learning and Teaching in Computing and Engineering (LaTiCE) Conference* (pp. 47–54). Macau: IEEE. doi:10.1109/LaTiCE.2013.34

Jackson, J. R. (1959). Learning from experience in business decision games. *California Management Review*, *1*(2), 92–107.

Kahneman, D. (2011). *Thinking, fast and slow*. New York: Farrar, Straus and Giroux.

Kumar, B., & Khurana, P. (2012). Gamification in education-learn computer programming with fun. *International Journal of Computers and Distributed Systems*, *2*(1), 46–53.

Li, W., Grossman, T., & Fitzmaurice, G. (2012, October). GamiCAD: A gamified tutorial system for first time autocad users. In *Proceedings of the 25th annual ACM symposium on user interface software and technology* (pp. 103–112). Cambridge, MA: ACM.

Mackie, D. M. (1987). Systematic and nonsystematic processing of majority and minority persuasive communications. *Journal of Personality and Social Psychology*, *53*, 41–52.

Mayo, M. J. (2009). Video games: A route to large-scale STEM education? *Science*, *323*(5910), 79–82. doi:10.1126/science.1166900

McGonigal, J. (2011). *Reality is broken: Why games make us better and how they can change the world*. New York, NY: Penguin.

Michael, D., & Chen, S. (2005). *Serious games: Games that educate, train, and inform*. Mason, OH: Course Technology, Cengage Learning PTR.

Milgram, S. (1992). In J. Sabini & M. Silver (Eds.), *Individual in a social world* (Second ed.). New York: McGraw-Hill.

Nah, F. F. H., Zeng, Q., Telaprolu, V. R., Ayyappa, A. P., & Eschenbrenner, B. (2014). Gamification of education: A review of literature. In F. H. H. Nah (Ed.), *Proceedings of 1st International Conference on Human-Computer Interaction in Business* (pp. 401–409). Crete, Greece: LNCS Springer.

Nicolao, L., Irwin, J., & Goodman, J. (2009). Happiness for sale: Do experiential purchases make consumers happier than material purchases? *Journal of Consumer Research*, *36*(2), 188–198. doi:10.1086/597049

Olbrish, K. (2011). *The ABC's of ARGs: Alternate reality games for learning*. eLearn Magazine. Retrieved from https://elearnmag.acm.org/archive.cfm?aid=2019544

Pine, B. J., & Gilmore, J. H. (1998). *Welcome to the experience economy*. Boston, MA: Harvard Business School Press. Retrieved from https://hbr.org/1998/07/welcome-to-the-experience-economy

Pine, B. J., & Gilmore, J. H. (1999). *The experience economy: Work is theatre & every business a stage*. Boston, MA: Harvard Business School Press.

Prensky, M. (2001). *Digital game-based learning*. New York: McGraw-Hill.

Quinn, C. N. (2005). *Engaging learning: Designing e-learning simulation games*. San Francisco, CA: Pfeiffer.

Randel, J. M., Morris, B. A., Wetzel, C. D., & Whitehill, B. V. (1992). The effectiveness of games for educational purposes: A review of recent research. Simulation & Gaming, 23(3), 261–276. Retrieved from doi:10.1177/1046878192233001.

Reeves, B., & Read, J. L. (2009). *Total engagement: How games and virtual worlds are changing the way people work and businesses compete*. Boston, MA: Harvard Business Press.

Schneider, W., & Shiffrin, R. M. (1977a). Controlled and automatic human information processing: 1. Detection, search, and attention. *Psychological Review, 84*, 1–66.

Schneider, W., & Shiffrin, R. M. (1977b). Controlled and automatic human information processing: 2. Perceptual learning, automatic attending and a general theory. *Psychological Review, 84*, 127–190.

Sitzmann, T. (2011). A meta-analytic examination of the instructional effectiveness of computer-based simulation games. *Personnel Psychology*, *64*(2), 489–528.

Smith, A. L., & Baker, L. (2011). Getting a clue: Creating student detectives and dragon slayers in your library. *Reference Services Review*, *39*(4), 628–642.

Stanovich, K. E. (1999). *Who is rational? Studies of individual differences in reasoning*. Mahwah, NJ: Lawrence Erlbaum Associates.

Su, C., & Cheng, C. (2015). A mobile gamification learning system for improving the learning motivation and achievements. *Journal of Computer Assisted Learning*, *31*(3), 268–286. doi:10.1111/jcal.12088

Thaler, R. H., & Sunstein, C. R. (2008). *Nudge: Improving decisions about health, wealth, and happiness*. New Haven, CT: Yale University Press.

Tversky, A., & Kahneman, D. (1974). Judgment under uncertainty: Heuristics and biases. *Science*, *185*(4157), 1124–1131. doi:10.1126/science.185.4157.1124

Ulrich, F., & Helms, N. H. (2017). Creating evaluation profiles for games designed to be fun: An interpretive framework for serious game mechanics. *Simulation & Gaming*. doi:10.1177/1046878117709841

van Grove, J. (2011). *Gamification: How competition is reinventing business, marketing & everyday life*. Retrieved from http://mashable.com/2011/07/28/gamification/#jwRDwxY4Okqq

Van Boven, L., & Gilovich, T. (2003). To do or to have?: That is the question. *Journal of Personality and Social Psychology*, *85*(6), 1193–1202. doi:10.1037/0022-3514.85.6.1193

Werbach, K., & Hunter, D. (2012). *For the win: How game thinking can revolutionize your business*. Philadelphia, PA: Wharton Digital Press.

Wilson, T. D. (2002). *Strangers to ourselves: Discovering the adaptive subconscious*. Cambridge, MA: Harvard University Press.

Yildirim, I. (2017). The effects of gamification-based teaching practices on student achievement and students' attitudes toward lessons. *The Internet and Higher Education, 33*, 86–92.

Zichermann, G., & Linder, J. (2013). *The gamification revolution: How leaders leverage game mechanics to crush the competition*. New York, NY: McGraw Hill.

Zyda, M. (2005). From visual simulation to virtual reality to games. *Computer*, *38*(9), 25–32. doi:10.1109/MC.2005.297

Chapter 5
Theories for Gamification in Learning and Education

Quest

Let's explore theories associated with gamification.
Let's understand concepts and principles of the theories.
Let's figure out how to apply the concepts and principles for learning and education.

5.1 Motivation Theory

Motivation is one of the most important factors that can influence the success of gamification (Sailer, Hense, Mandl, & Klevers, 2017). Motivation refers to the mental or emotional state that arouses an individual's behavioral or psychological change. It can be divided into two types: intrinsic and extrinsic motivation.

Intrinsic motivation is a motivation type that can be caused by an individual's own pleasure, curiosity, or interest. Ryan and Deci (2000) define intrinsic motivation as "the doing of an activity for its inherent satisfactions rather than for some separable consequence" (p. 56). It can be triggered to meet an individual's inherent satisfaction. Some researchers (Deci & Ryan, 2000; Taylor et al., 2014) have found intrinsic motivation to be more important than extrinsic motivation in academic achievement.

Extrinsic motivation is influenced by environmental and external factors, such as rewards, pressure, or punishment. According to Ryan and Deci (2000), extrinsic motivation is "a construct that pertains whenever an activity is done in order to attain some separable outcome" (p. 60). Not all students are intrinsically motivated in certain learning situations. Because of this practical problem, educators should consider using strategies for extrinsic motivation. Using care when designing for extrinsic motivation is necessary due to its inherent side effects. First, a student's motivation may not continue when the environmental or external factor disappears. Second, extrinsic motivation can decrease intrinsic motivation (Deci, Koestner, & Ryan, 1999; Deci, Koestner, Ryan, & Cameron, 2001; Kohn, 1993; Warneken, & Tomasello,

S. Kim et al., *Gamification in Learning and Education*, Advances in Game-Based Learning, DOI 10.1007/978-3-319-47283-6_5

2008). Thus, educators should be cautious when they use rewards or punishments to motivate their students.

It is hard to say that a motivation type is always more effective and important than the other. Students can be both intrinsically and extrinsically motivated (Lepper, Corpus, & Iyengar, 2005; Lepper, Greene, & Nisbett, 1973; Scanlon, Anderson, & Sweeney, 2016). Also, depending on the characteristics of learners, context, or instructional goal, one of the motivation types can be more effective than the other type. However, considering both motivation types simultaneously can be more beneficial than dealing with only one motivation type (Cerasoli, Nicklin, & Ford, 2014). This does not mean to mix a strategy for intrinsic motivation with another strategy for extrinsic motivation. Without understanding the characteristics of students and the possible effects, mixing motivational strategies is not a good idea since a mixed strategy can cause the strategy to be less effective or not work at all.

5.2 Self-Determination Theory

Self-determination theory is a macrotheory of motivation (Adams, Little, & Ryan, 2017; Deci & Ryan, 2008). It is based on an assumption that people's volition and motivation can be influenced by their environment, including social and cultural factors. According to self-determination theory, individuals tend to grow by their innate psychological needs: autonomy, competence, and relatedness.

To experience growth, individuals should

- Feel that they are able to control their behaviors and consequences
- Perceive that they have sufficient ability to accomplish tasks
- Have a sense that they belong to a group or interact with others

To encourage students' feeling of autonomy, educators can provide them as many choices as possible during instruction. For example, in selecting a topic for a group project, it can be more effective to allow students the opportunity to decide their project topic by themselves instead of their teacher deciding. Also, directing students to useful resources for the project would be a better strategy to facilitate autonomy than providing direct advice. When attempting to enhance student autonomy, educators should be cautious when also using extrinsic motivational strategies. Extrinsic rewards for a specific behavior that was intrinsically motivated can thwart autonomy (Deci, 1971; Hewett & Conway, 2016) and undermine intrinsic motivation (Deci et al., 1999, 2001; Warneken, & Tomasello, 2008).

Possessing competence is also associated with motivation. When individuals perceive that they are able to do something well, they can be intrinsically motivated (Deci & Ryan, 1985; Sari, Ekici, Soyer, & Eskiler, 2015). However, if a given task is too easy to complete, individuals hardly feel competent. To promote competence, the given task should be challenging, but can be completed with current ability (Park, Cha, Kwak, & Chen, 2017). This is similar with the flow mental state (Csikszentmihalyi, 1990) discussed in Chap. 2. When giving a task to students, teachers need to check if it is in accordance with students' abilities and challenging at the same time. If a student has difficulty in conducting the task, the teacher can scaffold the student instead of providing an immediate solution. When provided a direct answer, a student is more likely to lose competence. Also, while positive feedback on a student's performance can promote competence and intrinsic motivation (Vallerand & Reid, 1988), negative feedback can reduce competence and intrinsic motivation (Weidinger, Spinath, & Steinmayr, 2016). Thus, educators should be cautious in the way they provide students' performance feedback.

Relatedness is another significant psychological condition to experience growth (Altintas, De Benedetto & Gallouj, 2017). Students can be more intrinsically motivated when they perceive relatedness from their teachers (Sparks, Dimmock, Lonsdale, & Jackson, 2016) and peers (Cox, Duncheon, & McDavid, 2009). Also, sense of relatedness to parents influences academic performance (King, 2015) and classroom engagement (Furrer & Skinner, 2003). When perceiving supportive and warm behaviors from teachers, peers, or parents, a student can feel positive relatedness and be motivated.

5.3 Achievement Goal Theory

Achievement goal theory (Dweck & Leggett, 1988; Elliott & Dweck, 1988) suggests individuals can be motivated by their belief or desire to achieve a specific goal. Achievement goal theory consists of two major goal types: mastery goals and performance goals (Hamstra, Yperen, Wisse, & Sassenberg, 2014; Nicholls, 1984; Pekrun, Cusack, Murayama, Elliot, & Thomas, 2014), also called task-involved goals and ego-involved goals (Eccles & Wigfield, 2002).

Mastery goals are the desire to acquire abilities that are required to conduct a task or understand a concept. Individuals with mastery goals focus on learning themselves, competence development, and self-improvement. On the contrary, performance goals are the desire to show higher achievements than other people. Those with performance goals are interested more in social comparison and its results (Seifert, 2004).

Individuals with mastery goals tend to show high self-efficacy, quantity and quality of self-regulation, and academic achievement (Linnenbrink, 2005; Robinson, Palmer, & Bub, 2016). Although performance goals can also influence achievements (Pintrich, 2000; van Yperen, Blaga, & Postmes, 2014), educators should be careful when considering the use of performance goals for their instruction. Performance goals can negatively influence self-efficacy and motivation (Schunk & Mullen, 2012). Also, depending on student types, the effects of performance goals may vary. For example, in competitive learning environments, performance goals are more effective to boys or older students than girls and younger ones (Midgley & Kaplan, 2001).

It might be natural to think that mastery goals are more ideal than performance goals and that students with mastery goals can achieve more than those with performance goals. However, the achievement goals are not fixed. They are dynamic and can be changed over time. For example, students with mastery goals during most of the semester can create performance goals near exam time (Pintrich, 2000). Moreover, there are few empirical studies showing superior effects of mastery goals over performance goals (Darnon, Butera, & Harackiewicz, 2007).

In education, how do educators evaluate students' achievements? Educators are probably familiar with criterion-referenced tests and norm-referenced tests. The former can be a means to see if an individual's mastery goals are achieved while the latter can be an instrument used to determine a student's achievement of performance goals. Both of these test types have been used to assess students' achievements for a long time. Depending on the purpose and need of each evaluation, an optimal test type or a combined type has been used. Therefore, the answer to the question depends on the instructional goals, the learning context, and the learners. Because of this, educators should not focus on the selection of one type of achievement goal over the other. Before deciding to use one of the achievement goal types or both, it is necessary to understand learning environments (Linnenbrink, 2005), possible side-effects (Kaplan & Maehr, 1999), and the characteristics of students.

5.4 Social Learning Theory and Situated Learning Theory

Social learning theory (SLT) posits that people can learn by observing others, their behaviors, and the results of the observed behaviors. As explained by SLT, learning incorporates social interaction as well as the cognitive processing. Bandura (1977) suggests four principles of social learning, which are attention, retention, reproduction, and motivation. For effective social learning, according to Bandura (1977), an individual should pay attention to other people's behaviors, remember the observed behaviors, be able to reproduce the behaviors, and have a motivation to do the same behaviors.

In education, a student can learn by observing other students' behaviors and the consequence of the behaviors. Thus, creating a learning environment that provides opportunities to students to observe a model student is important in social learning. The model for social learning does not need to be limited to peers. It can be teachers, parents, or someone else in and out of classrooms. Students sometimes find their models in learning materials. For example, a student can observe an actor's behavior and its consequences from a documentary film. Though there is less social interaction in such learning materials, students still can learn through modeling the behaviors in the learning materials. When it is hard to find an appropriate model, educators can use learning materials that facilitate social relationships and modeling. Simulation games are another good example of such learning materials. Within the games, players can learn by interacting with and modeling other players or game characters.

Similar to Bandura's social learning theory, situated learning theory is also based on the assumption that learning occurs through social interaction. Lave (1988, 1991) claims that learning is situated. This means learning is inseparable from the activity, context, and culture. According to situated learning theory, knowledge is socially constructed and closely associated with contexts.

Learning that lacks authentic contexts makes its application to the real world more difficult (Collins, Brown, & Newman, 1989). Have you ever tried to use role playing, scenario-based learning, or field trips as learning activities? The fundamental assumption of role playing, scenario-based learning, and field trips is that individuals can learn better in the environment and context in which the learning can be applied. This assumption is well expressed in the following core principles of situated learning theory.

- Knowledge needs to be presented in authentic contexts.
- Social interaction and collaboration are required for effective learning.

Brown, Collins, and Duguid (1989) have further developed situated learning theory and suggest cognitive apprenticeship to describe learning through guided experience in a field. The researchers argue that social construction of knowledge and social interaction can promote learning and cognitive apprenticeship can help novices' enculturation by providing an authentic environment to engage students in a community of practice. Coaches, mentors, or peers in the field can facilitate novices' learning and enculturation.

Legitimate peripheral participation (Lave & Wenger, 1991) is one of the methods which support cognitive apprenticeship. It is a concept describing how novices in a field can become an expert by participating in different levels of activities, ranging from peripheral and simple activities to advanced and complex activities. The novices in a field begin their activities with peripheral ones and gradually approach to the advanced and core activities of the field.

5.5 Feedback

Since Thorndike's study (Thorndike, 1911), feedback has been popularly studied in many disciplines because of its effects on performance. Feedback is a verbal or nonverbal message reflecting an evaluation result on performance. It can be used for guiding individuals, or sometimes other than human, to an intended behavior or state. In education, feedback is one of the most important means to facilitate learning (Brookhart, 2017).

Feedback can be divided into positive feedback and negative feedback in terms of the mood of the feedback content. While positive feedback is supportive, encouraging, and emphasizing on strengths, negative feedback focuses on what and how to improve weaknesses and poorly performed areas. Positive feedback is effective in changing behaviors (Burgers, Eden, van Engelenburg, & Buningh, 2015; Ryan, Ormond, Imwold, & Rotunda, 2002; Zhu, Kraut, & Kittur, 2012). Negative feedback can be also effective in learning if it is delivered with a clear message on the ways to improve rather than just description on poor performance (Zhuang, Feng & Liao, 2017). Also, the effect of positive and negative feedback can vary depending on the level of expertise. While experts can be motivated by negative feedback, novices tend to be more motivated by positive feedback (Fishbach, Eyal, & Finkelstein, 2010). Feedback can be also classified by who evaluates performance. From this viewpoint, there can be internal and external feedback. Some researchers, especially behaviorists, have paid relatively more attention to external feedback than internal feedback. However, individuals can monitor goals, knowledge, skills, beliefs, and strategies within their cognitive system (Butler & Winne, 1995) and generate feedback for themselves (Moos, 2014). From the viewpoint of feedback timing, there can be immediate feedback and delayed feedback. Immediate feedback is usually more effective than delayed feedback except for the case of acquisition of test contents (Kulik & Kulik, 1988; Price, Martella, Marchand-Martella, & Cleanthous, 2002; Scheeler, Ruhl, & McAfee, 2004). Simulation-based learning, serious game-based learning, or other learning types using information technologies can support immediate feedback.

A medium as a means to deliver feedback should be carefully selected. Feedback can be delivered through various media, such as oral communication, gestures, facial expressions, texts, or multimedia. Depending on the context and conditions of an instruction, the media for delivering feedback can be different. In some cases, feedback in text can be more convenient, efficient, and able to include specific information than video feedback (Borup, West, & Thomas, 2015). In some other cases, feedback using recorded audio can be effective (Hennessy & Forrester, 2014; Morrell et al., 1974). To improve the effect of feedback, teachers may consider using fading strategy. Fading is a method that gradually decreases the level of help that are necessary to learn or master a task. Fading promotes students' reflection and internalize what they are learning and cognitively using. Schunk and Rice (1993) argue that students who are provided feedback with fading strategies can use comprehension strategies more and achieve higher outcomes than those who are not.

Feedback is not always effective (Kluger & DeNisi, 1998; Okita, Turkay, Kim, & Murai, 2013). Feedback can be effective when it correctly reflects students' performance and guides them to improve their performance. Also, depending on circumstances, providing elaborations through instruction can be more effective than delivering feedback on incorrect understanding and poor performance area, especially when students are inefficient and not proficient at applying feedback (Hattie & Timperley, 2007). Thus, educators should understand the characteristics of students and context to design feedback.

References

Adams, N., Little, T. D., & Ryan, R. M. (2017). Self-determination theory. In M. L. Wehmeyer, K. A. Shogren, T. D. Little, & S. J. Lopez (Eds.), *Development of self-determination through the life-course* (pp. 47–54). Dordrecht, Netherlands: Springer.

Altintas, E., De Benedetto, G., & Gallouj, K. (2017). Adaptation to nursing home: The role of leisure activities in light of motivation and relatedness. *Archives of Gerontology and Geriatrics*, *70*, 8–13.

Bandura, A. (1977). *Social learning theory*. Englewood Cliffs, NJ: Prentice Hall.

Borup, J., West, R. E., & Thomas, R. (2015). The impact of text versus video communication on instructor feedback in blended courses. *Educational Technology Research and Development, 63*(2), 161–184. doi:10.1007/s11423-015-9367-8

Brookhart, S. M. (2017). *How to give effective feedback to your students* (2nd ed.). Alexandria, VA: ASCD.

Brown, J. S., Collins, A., & Duguid, S. (1989). Situated cognition and the culture of learning. *Educational Researcher, 18*(1), 32–42.

Burgers, C., Eden, A., van Engelenburg, M. D., & Buningh, S. (2015). How feedback boosts motivation and play in a brain-training game. *Computers in Human Behavior, 48*, 94–103. doi:10.1016/j.chb.2015.01.038

Butler, D. L., & Winne, P. H. (1995). Feedback and self-regulated learning: A theoretical synthesis. *Review of Educational Research, 65*(3), 245–281. doi:10.2307/1170684

Cerasoli, C. P., Nicklin, J. M., & Ford, M. T. (2014). Intrinsic motivation and extrinsic incentives jointly predict performance: A 40-year meta-analysis. *Psychological Bulletin, 140*(4), 980.

Collins, A., Brown, J. S., & Newman, S. E. (1989). Cognitive apprenticeship: Teaching the craft of reading, writing, and mathematics. In L. B. Resnick (Ed.), *Knowing, learning, and instruction: Essays in honor of Robert Glaser* (pp. 453–494). Hillsdale, NJ: Lawrence Erlbaum Associates.

Cox, A., Duncheon, N., & McDavid, L. (2009). Peers and teachers as sources of relatedness perceptions, motivation, and affective responses in physical education. *Research Quarterly for Exercise and Sport, 80*(4), 765–773. doi:10.1080/02701367.2009.10599618

Csikszentmihalyi, M. (1990). *Flow: The psychology of optimal experience*. New York, NY: Harper & Row

Darnon, C., Butera, F., & Harackiewicz, J. M. (2007). Achievement goals in social interactions: Learning with mastery vs. performance goals. *Motivation and Emotion, 31*(1), 61–70.

Deci, E. L. (1971). Effects of externally mediated rewards on intrinsic motivation. *Journal of Personality and Social Psychology, 18*(1), 105–115.

Deci, E. L., Koestner, R., & Ryan, R. M. (1999). A meta-analytic review of experiments examining the effects of extrinsic rewards on intrinsic motivation. *Psychological Bulletin, 125*(6), 627–668. doi:10.1037/0033-2909.125.6.627

Deci, E. L., Koestner, R., Ryan, R. M., & Cameron, J. (2001). Extrinsic rewards and intrinsic motivation in education: Reconsidered once again. *Review of Educational Research, 71*(1), 1–27.

Deci, E. L., & Ryan, R. M. (1985). *Intrinsic motivation and self-determination in human behavior*. New York, NY: Plenum.

Deci, E. L., & Ryan, R. M. (2000). The "what" and "why" of goal pursuits: Human needs and the self-determination of behavior. *Psychological Inquiry, 11*, 227–268. doi:10.1207/S15327965PLI1104_01

Deci, E. L., & Ryan, R. M. (2008). Self-determination theory: A macrotheory of human motivation, development, and health. *Canadian Psychology/Psychologie Canadienne, 49*(3), 182–185.

Dweck, C. S., & Leggett, E. L. (1988). A social-cognitive approach to motivation and personality. *Psychological Review, 95*(2), 256–273. doi:10.1037/0033-295X.95.2.256

Eccles, J. S., & Wigfield, A. (2002). Motivational beliefs, values, and goals. *Annual Review of Psychology, 53*(1), 109–132. doi:10.1146/annurev.psych.53.100901.135153

Elliott, E. S., & Dweck, C. S. (1988). Goals: An approach to motivation and achievement. *Journal of Personality and Social Psychology, 54*(1), 5–12.

Fishbach, A., Eyal, T., & Finkelstein, S. R. (2010). How positive and negative feedback motivate goal pursuit: Feedback motivates goal pursuit. *Social and Personality Psychology Compass, 4*(8), 517–530. doi:10.1111/j.1751-9004.2010.00285.x

Furrer, C., & Skinner, E. (2003). Sense of relatedness as a factor in children's academic engagement and performance. *Journal of Educational Psychology, 95*(1), 148–162. doi:10.1037/0022-0663.95.1.148

Hamstra, M. R. W., van Yperen, N. W., Wisse, B., & Sassenberg, K. (2014). Transformational and transactional leadership and followers' achievement goals. *Journal of Business and Psychology, 29*(3), 413–425.

Hattie, J., & Timperley, H. (2007). The power of feedback. *Review of Educational Research, 77*(1), 81–112. Retrieved from http://www.jstor.org.ezproxy.lib.vt.edu/stable/4624888

Hennessy, C., & Forrester, G. (2014). Developing a framework for effective audio feedback: A case study. *Assessment & Evaluation in Higher Education, 39*(7), 777–789. doi:10.1080/02602938.2013.870530

Hewett, R., & Conway, N. (2016). The undermining effect revisited: The salience of everyday verbal rewards and self-determined motivation. *Journal of Organizational Behavior, 37*(3), 436–455. doi:10.1002/job.2051

Kaplan, A., & Maehr, M. L. (1999). Achievement goals and student well-being. *Contemporary Educational Psychology, 24*(4), 330–358. doi:10.1006/ceps.1999.0993

King, R. B. (2015). Sense of relatedness boosts engagement, achievement, and well-being: A latent growth model study. *Contemporary Educational Psychology, 42*, 26–38. doi:10.1016/j.cedpsych.2015.04.002

Kluger, A. N., & DeNisi, A. (1998). Feedback interventions: Toward the understanding of a double-edged sword. *Current Directions in Psychological Science, 7*(3), 67–72. doi:10.1111/1467-8721.ep10772989

Kohn, A. (1993). *Punished by rewards*. Boston, MA: Houghton Mifflin.

Kulik, J. A., & Kulik, C. C. (1988). Timing of feedback and verbal learning. *Review of Educational Research, 58*(1), 79–97. doi:10.3102/00346543058001079

Lave, J. (1988). *Cognition in practice: Mind, mathematics, and culture in everyday life*. Cambridge, UK: Cambridge University Press.

Lave, J. (1991). Situating learning in communities of practice. *Perspectives on socially shared cognition, 2*, 63–82.

Lave, J., & Wenger, E. (1991). *Situated learning: Legitimate peripheral participation*. Cambridge, UK: Cambridge University Press.

Lepper, M. R., Corpus, J. H., & Iyengar, S. S. (2005). Intrinsic and extrinsic motivational orientations in the classroom: Age differences and academic correlates. *Journal of Educational Psychology, 97*, 184–196.

Lepper, M. R., Greene, D., & Nisbett, R. E. (1973). Undermining children's intrinsic interest with extrinsic reward: A test of the "overjustification" hypothesis. *Journal of Personality and Social Psychology, 28*(1), 129–137.

Linnenbrink, E. A. (2005). The dilemma of performance-approach goals The use of multiple goal contexts to promote students' motivation and learning. *Journal of Educational Psychology, 97*(2), 197–213. doi:10.1037/0022-0663.97.2.197

Midgley, C., & Kaplan, A. (2001). Performance-approach goals: Good for what, for whom, under what circumstances, and at what cost? *Journal of Educational Psychology, 93*(1), 77–86.

Moos, D. C. (2014). Setting the stage for the metacognition during hypermedia learning: What motivation constructs matter? *Computers & Education, 70*, 128–137. doi:10.1016/j.compedu.2013.08.014

Morrell, J. E., Walker, C. R., Loughery, C., Funk, J., Ruoff, G., & Proger, B. B. (1974). Cognitive and affective effects of audio-programed electronic feedback and oral teacher feedback. *AV Communication Review, 22*(3), 303–315.

Nicholls, J. G. (1984). Achievement motivation: Conceptions of ability, subjective experience, task choice, and performance. *Psychological Review, 91*, 328–346.

Okita, S. Y., Turkay, S., Kim, M., & Murai, Y. (2013). Learning by teaching with virtual peers and the effects of technological design choices on learning. *Computers & Education, 63*, 176–196. doi:10.1016/j.compedu.2012.12.005

Park, K., Cha, M., Kwak, H., & Chen, K. T. (2017, April). Achievement and friends: Key factors of player retention vary across player levels in online multiplayer games. *Proceedings of the 26th International Conference on World Wide Web Companion* (pp. 445–453). Perth, Australia: International World Wide Web Conferences Steering Committee.

Pekrun, R., Cusack, A., Murayama, K., Elliot, A. J., & Thomas, K. (2014). The power of anticipated feedback: Effects on students' achievement goals and achievement emotions. *Learning and Instruction, 29*, 115–124. doi:10.1016/j.learninstruc.2013.09.002

Pintrich, P. R. (2000). Multiple goals, multiple pathways: The role of goal orientation in learning and achievement. *Journal of Educational Psychology, 92*(3), 544–555. doi:10.1037/0022-0663.92.3.544

Price, A., Martella, R., Marchand-Martella, N., & Cleanthous, C. (2002). A comparison of immediate feedback delivered via an FM headset versus delayed feedback on the inappropriate verbalizations of a student with ADHD. *Education and Treatment of Children, 25*, 159–171.

Robinson, L. E., Palmer, K. K., & Bub, K. L. (2016). Effect of the children's health activity motor program on motor skills and self-regulation in head start preschoolers: An efficacy trial. *Frontiers in Public Health, 4*, 173. Retrieved from http://doi.org/10.3389/fpubh.2016.00173

Ryan, R. M., & Deci, E. L. (2000). Intrinsic and extrinsic motivations: Classic definitions and new directions. *Contemporary Educational Psychology, 25*(1), 54–67. doi:10.1006/ceps.1999.1020

Ryan, S., Ormond, T., Imwold, C., & Rotunda, R. J. (2002). The effects of a public address system on the off-task behavior of elementary physical education students. *Journal of Applied Behavior Analysis, 35*(3), 305–308. doi:10.1901/jaba.2002.35-305

Sailer, M., Hense, J., Mandl, H., & Klevers, M. (2017). Fostering development of work competencies and motivation via gamification. In M. Mulder (Ed.), *Competence-based vocational and professional education: Bridging the worlds of work and education* (pp. 795–818). Cham, Switzerland: Springer International Publishing AG.

Sari, İ., Ekici, S., Soyer, F., & Eskiler, E. (2015). Does self-confidence link to motivation? A study in field hockey athletes. *Journal of Human Sport and Exercise, 10*(1), 24–35.

Scanlon, D. M., Anderson, K. L., & Sweeney, J. M. (2016). *Early intervention for reading difficulties: The interactive strategies approach* (2nd ed.). New York, NY: The Guilford Press.

Scheeler, M. C., Ruhl, K. L., & McAfee, J. K. (2004). Providing performance feedback to teachers: A review. *Teacher Education and Special Education, 27*(4), 396–407. doi:10.1177/088840640402700407

Schunk, D. H., & Mullen, C. A. (2012). Self-efficacy as an engaged learner. In S. L. Christenson, A. L. Reschly, & C. Wylie (Eds.), *Handbook of research on student engagement*. Boston, MA: Springer. doi:10.1007/978-1-4614-2018-7_10

Schunk, D. H., & Rice, J. M. (1993). Strategy fading and progress feedback: Effects on self-efficacy and comprehension among students receiving remedial reading services. *The Journal of Special Education, 27*(3), 257–276. doi:10.1177/002246699302700301

Seifert, T. (2004). Understanding student motivation. *Educational Research, 46*(2), 137–149. doi:10.1080/0013188042000222421

Sparks, C., Dimmock, J., Lonsdale, C., & Jackson, B. (2016). Modeling indicators and outcomes of students' perceived teacher relatedness support in high school physical education. *Psychology of Sport and Exercise, 26*, 71–82. doi:10.1016/j.psychsport.2016.06.004

Taylor, G., Jungert, T., Mageau, G. A., Schattke, K., Dedic, H., Rosenfield, S., & Koestner, R. (2014). A self-determination theory approach to predicting school achievement over time: The unique role of intrinsic motivation. *Contemporary Educational Psychology, 39*(4), 342–358.

Thorndike, E. L. (1911). *Animal intelligence: Experimental studies*. New York, NY: Macmillan.

Vallerand, R. J., & Reid, G. (1988). On the relative effects of positive and negative verbal feedback on males' and females' intrinsic motivation. *Canadian Journal of Behavioural Science, 20*(3), 239–250. doi:10.1037/h0079930

van Yperen, N. W., Blaga, M., & Postmes, T. (2014). A meta-analysis of self-reported achievement goals and nonself-report performance across three achievement domains (work, sports, and education). *PloS One, 9*(4), e93594. doi:10.1371/journal.pone.0093594

Warneken, F., & Tomasello, M. (2008). Extrinsic rewards undermine altruistic tendencies in 20-month-olds. *Developmental Psychology, 44*(6), 1785–1788. doi:10.1037/a0013860

Weidinger, A. F., Spinath, B., & Steinmayr, R. (2016). Why does intrinsic motivation decline following negative feedback? The mediating role of ability self-concept and its moderation by goal orientations. *Learning and Individual Differences, 47*, 117–128. doi:10.1016/j.lindif.2016.01.003

Zhu, H., Kraut, R., & Kittur, A. (2012, February). *Effectiveness of shared leadership in online communities*. Paper presented at the ACM 2012 Conference on Computer Supported Cooperative Work. doi:10.1145/2145204.2145269.

Zhuang, Y., Feng, W., & Liao, Y. (2017). Want more? Learn less: Motivation affects adolescents learning from negative feedback. *Frontiers in Psychology, 8*(76), 1–10.

Chapter 6
Students' Perception of Gamification in Learning and Education

Quest
Let's see how our students perceive gamification in learning and education settings.
Let's find out how people behave in games.
Let's understand why some game players misbehave within a game.

6.1 Types of Fun in a Game

In 1981, Malone developed a theory of intrinsically motivating instruction (Malone, 1981). For developing the theory, the researcher reviewed literature on highly motivating computer games and theories of intrinsic motivation. In the study, the researcher categorized the elements making games fun into three groups: challenge, fantasy, and curiosity. Lepper (1988) more focused on instructional design in his study investigating intrinsic motivation, and argued for four design principles for motivational instruction which are control, challenge, curiosity, and contextualization.

Korhonen, Montola, and Arrasvunori (2009) investigated the types of playful experiences that can be found in playing recent games, such as "Grand Theft Auto IV," "The Sims 2," and "Spore." In the study, the researchers suggested the Playful Experience (PLEX) framework in which the playful experiences in games were categorized into 20 types: captivation, challenge, competition, completion, control, discovery, eroticism, exploration, expression, fantasy, fellowship, nurture, relaxation, sadism, sensation, simulation, subversion, suffering, sympathy, and thrill. Table 6.1 illustrates the 20 playful experiences in the PLEX framework.

Gamers can experience various fun types from the game. Some people prefer a particular fun type to other fun types. Kim (2013) investigated students' preferences of a fun type using the PLEX framework and found out that students prefer challenge, exploration, relaxation, completion, and discovery to suffering, sadism, and control.

Kim (2013) also found that gender differences occur in the preference of one type of fun over another while playing a game. Male students prefer challenge,

S. Kim et al., *Gamification in Learning and Education*, Advances in Game-Based Learning, DOI 10.1007/978-3-319-47283-6_6

Table 6.1 20 playful experiences in the PLEX framework

Experience	Description
Captivation	Gamers forget their surroundings and engage in a game
Challenge	Gamers need to learn new skills or improve their current skills to solve a problem in a task. They can test the abilities of their characters with challenge
Competition	Gamers need to compete with other gamers, virtual competitors, or gamers themselves for achieving a goal
Completion	Gamers can finish a major task when they complete required quests and missions. Gamers can feel relaxation when they reach the completion
Control	Gamers can control other gamers, game characters, and surrounding situations with their power and skills. They can command game characters to achieve a goal, regulate situations including available resources, and dominate other gamers
Discovery	Gamers can find a new or unknown place, solution, or object. Some games include maps and navigation devices in the game. Gamers sometimes can collaborate with other gamers for discovery
Eroticism	Gamers can experience sexual feelings and affection by interacting with game characters or other gamers
Exploration	Gamers can explore and investigate an object or situation. They sometimes explore the relationships between objects or characters. In some games, exploration is necessary to complete missions
Expression	Games express their identity by manifesting themselves. In many games, gamers can use an avatar as a device for their interaction. Gamers can decorate the avatar using clothes, hats, shoes, weapons, hairs, or physical characteristics of the avatar
Fantasy	Through playing games, gamers can experience something that may not exist in real world. Gamers can experience stories, characters, and situations that they have never thought or believed
Fellowship	Gamers can experience fellowship, communality, and friendship by communicating or collaborating with other gamers. Some games require gamers to collaborate with other gamers to complete a mission or receive a reward
Nurture	Gamers can experience fun by taking care of game characters, other gamers, or themselves. Some gamers perceive the nurture itself as a fun, but some others think the nurture as a means to experience other types of fun, such as completion and discovery
Relaxation	Gamers can feel relaxed while playing the game since games include stress-free or peaceful situations, to not to make gamers exhausted. Continuous intense situations from conducting challenging quests and competing with other gamers can make gamers to stop playing the game. Relaxation is different from pausing the game. Gamers can experience relaxation while they dominate the situation within the game
Sadism	Some gamers experience fun by harassing and teasing game characters and other gamers. In some games, sadism is a means to complete a quest
Sensation	Gamers can experience fun by sensing a stimulus. Many games use visual and auditory stimuli, but the type of senses does not need to be limited. With wearable devices or other new technologies including something we have not imagined so far, games can extend the type of sensation that gamers can experience within the game
Simulation	Gamers can experience a simulated situation in the game. Some gamers feel fun from the simulated situation. Functional games and simulation games focus on this kind of fun. Gamers can drive tanks, submarines, fighters, and spaceships in functional games and simulation games

(continued)

Table 6.1 (continued)

Experience	Description
Subversion	Gamers can feel fun by breaking social rules and conducting something against social expectation. In some games, gamers trade drugs and rob a shop. These kinds of quests can be included to gamers with fun of subversion
Suffering	Gamers can experience embarrassment, frustration, stress, anger, and disappointment in the game. No gamers like these experiences, but these are necessary for improving skills or completing a quest in some games. Some of the gamers who experienced suffering can feel larger level of fun when they successfully complete a mission
Sympathy	Gamers can have the same emotional state as the game characters or other gamers have. To make gamers have more sympathy in the game, forming fellowship can be considered first since the level of sympathy is influenced by the level of fellowship
Thrill	Gamers can experience fun from taking a risk or getting threatened within the game. Gamers can feel this kind of fun more in racing games and shooting games

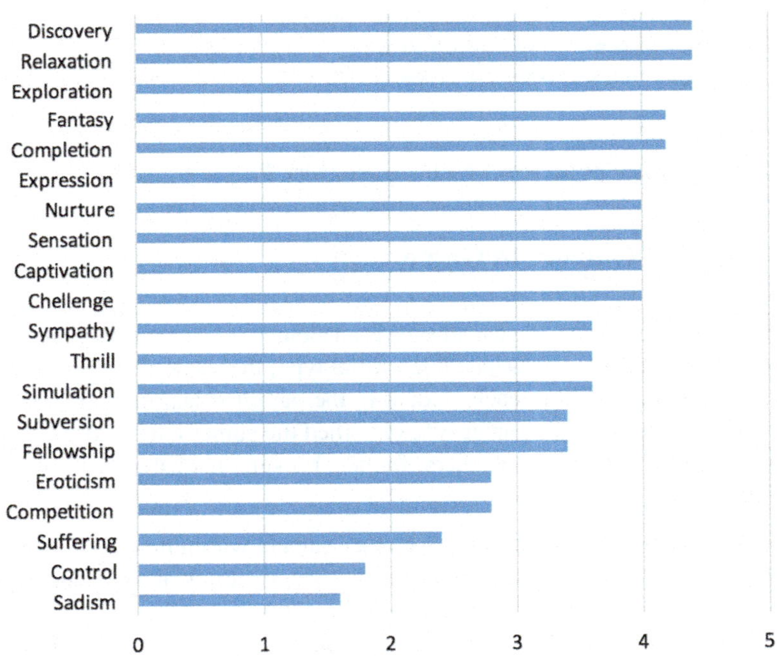

Fig. 6.1 Female students' preference on fun from game (Kim, 2013, p. 6)

completion, exploration, and simulation, however, female students prefer exploration, relaxation, discovery, completion, and fantasy. The major difference by gender appeared in expression, fantasy, and nurture (see Figs. 6.1 and 6.2).

Kim (2013) suggested that the gender difference on fun preferences should be considered for gamifying learning and education. Although a gamified course using nurture and fantasy may be effective for female students, male students may feel bored.

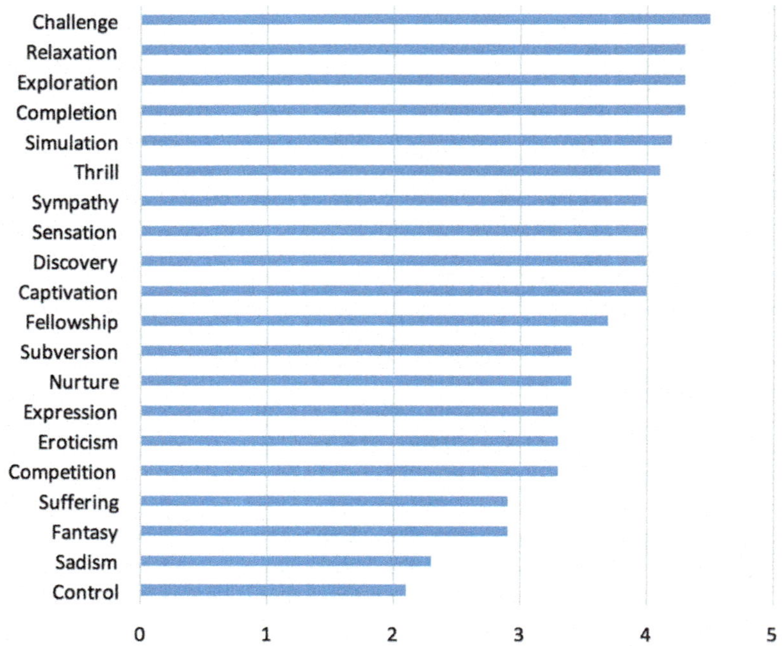

Fig. 6.2 Male students' preference on fun from game (Kim, 2013, p. 6)

6.2 Types of Gamers in Game

In addition to the fun type, the gamer type is an element to be considered in gamifying learning and education. Depending on the type, the game designer or teacher can assign different roles to each student in the gamified learning and education. Bartle's (2005) study on the gamer type classified the gamer into eight types: griefers, opportunists, politicians, planners, friends, hackers, networkers, and scientists (see Fig. 6.3).

- *Griefer type gamers* harass and tease other gamers within the game. They want to get a reputation no matter what the other gamers think about them. Some of the griefer type gamers enjoy getting a bad reputation.
- *Opportunist type gamers* explore the game and take a chance when they see it. They tend to look around the game without a specific objective. When facing obstacles and challenges in the game, this type of gamer is more likely to try to avoid them rather than removing and overcoming them.
- *Politician type gamers* strategically play the game to achieve a long-term goal. Their behaviors are based on foresight and forethought. They sometimes manipulate other gamers for their goals. They enjoy getting a good reputation.

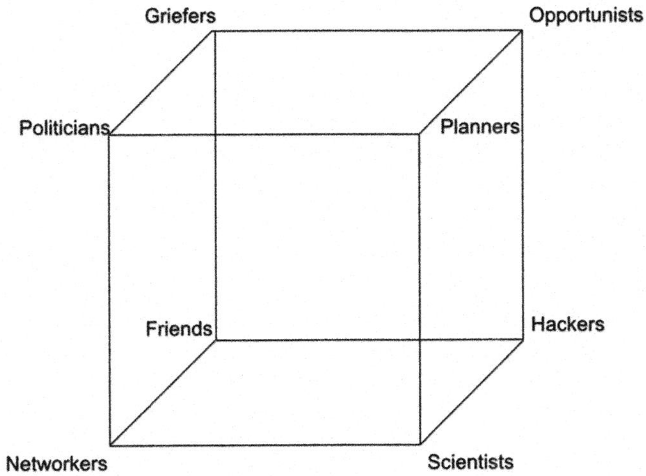

Fig. 6.3 Bartle's gamer type

- *Planner type gamers* are also very strategic to achieve a goal. They set a goal before taking an action within the game. They check their progress and status while playing the game.
- *Friend type gamers* focus on friendship with other gamers. They prefer keeping existing friendship to making a new relationship with another gamer. They try to deeply understand their friends. They are sympathetic with their friends' mistakes.
- *Hacker type gamers* do what they want to do. They are usually not reluctant to do something they are interested in. They are also interested in a new object, event, and place. Many of them make a decision by their intuition.
- *Networker type gamers* enjoy making a new friend. They evaluate their friends and the relationship and decide if the friendship is beneficial or not.
- *Scientist type gamers* are interested in the causes and reasons of an event and a phenomenon. They systematically learn about the game and how to play the game well. They sometimes try to do experiments during the game.

6.3 Handling Griefers and Rule Breakers

Griefers and rule breakers are similar in that both may influence a teacher's attempt to gamify learning, however, the purposes of their behaviors are different. While the griefers gain pleasure from harassing and teasing other gamers, over advancing in the game, the rule breakers demonstrate similar behavior, but with the purpose of making their mission easier or showing other gamers their abilities.

6.3.1 Griefers

Some people do not understand what the griefers are exactly. Griefers more focus on harassing and teasing other gamers than achieving a higher level or attaining more points (Ladanyi & Doyle-Portillo, 2017). Some griefers record their games, showing other gamers' reactions to their harassment and teasing in order to show off to their audiences.

The griefer type gamer is not a new concept. Some people may think the griefer type gamer had emerged when MMORGs became popular. The griefer type gamers, however, existed in the 1980s, which was an era of the MUD games. According to Google Trends (www.google.com/trends/), the search for "griefer" has increased over time. It is not unreasonable to speculate that the number of griefers and the number of their victims have also increased. Some researchers (Davies, 2006; Edge, 2013; Lin & Sun, 2005; Victoria, 2011) have investigated the behavioral patterns of griefers. The following lists some of their behavioral patterns:

- Block a road or path to make other gamers cannot pass it.
- Obstruct other gamers' view in a shooting game.
- Kill the game character that another gamer is about to kill and take the game point.
- Destroy the item that another gamer made.
- Pretend to be a game administrator or another gamer by using a plausible game ID or avatar.
- Provide teammates with false information or waste the resources in a team play.
- Use a violent or uncomfortable picture for the gamer profile.
- Repeatedly kill other gamers when they begin or start over the game.
- Intentionally attract other gamers to make them encounter a game character that is hard to kill or encounter a difficult mission.
- Insult or blame at other gamers without any reasons.
- Repeatedly send unnecessary messages to teammates or other gamers.

Some griefers target new and weak gamers, since they are more likely to achieve their goals with them (Edge, 2013). Their behaviors are sometimes considered as a crime within the game. To prevent the crime, games employ a means, similar to real-world police. Some games use a game master to find griefers and apply penalties. Davies (2006) argued that it is more effective for gamers to police themselves rather than the game manufacturer or a game master.

Woolfolk (2006) classified aggressive gaming behavior in educational settings into two types: instrumental aggression and hostile aggression. The purpose of instrumental aggression is to hurt other students to achieve a particular goal rather than to cause pain. Instrumental aggression includes both psychological and physical aggression. On the other hand, hostile aggression is an intentional action mainly to make other students feel pain. Hostile aggression includes overt aggression and relational aggression. While the purpose of overt aggression is to physically hurt other students or damage their things and works, relational aggression is an act of aggression that intends to disconnect the social relationships of other students. Berk (2011) insists that overt aggression can be found more in male students than in female students, and relational aggression occurs more frequently in female students than in male students.

Griefers' behaviors are closer to overt aggression than relational aggression or instrumental aggression because their purpose is to psychologically hurt other gamers or damage other gamers' progress. Then why do griefers show overt aggression in the game? Since there are many griefers who harass and tease the beginner in the game, personal revenge cannot be a main reason. They may enjoy tormenting other players and consider it one of the playful experiences in the game.

Broidy et al. (2003) claim that male students who showed aggressive behavior as elementary school students may repeatedly commit violence and delinquency during an adolescent period. In gamification, failure to manage the griefer issue may lead to serious problems.

Overaggression is not new to game-play, and griefers have existed for a long time. For managing the griefer issue, the following should be considered:

- Prevention: Minimize the chance for the griefer to affect the gamified learning and education. For example, let's assume that a teacher distributed a list of books that are in the school library to her students and asked them to read one of the books on the list by next week. For this assignment, the griefer will try to check out as many books as possible to put other students in trouble. In this case, the teacher can distribute a different book list to each student to minimize the chance of hindrance by the griefer.
- Discovery: MMORPGs employ a device to report griefers. The device includes game masters and gamers (Davies, 2006). The device can be applied for gamification for learning and education. A teacher can observe students' behaviors and find griefers. Students can report griefers to their teacher. So, teachers should inform their students of the device at the beginning of gamified learning and education.
- Recovery: If a student has been victimized by a griefer, the teacher should try to recover the student's status before the grief. The teacher can consider giving the student additional points, badges, or a level to recover the student's status. On the other hand, a penalty for the griefer should be imposed. The teacher can consider collecting the benefits that the griefer took and impose additional penalties. For the additional penalties, the teacher should weigh the level of damage and the intention.
- Correction: It is necessary to find the reason of the grief. Teachers or designers should review the elements used in the gamified learning and education to establish what was weak to the grief. If the weakness cannot be corrected, due to the structure and mechanism of the gamified learning and education, the teacher should guide his or her students to not use the weakness as a griefer would and notify them of penalties for griefer behavior in the beginning of the class or course.

6.3.2 Rule Breakers

While griefers pursue sadism, rule breakers try to take advantages by bending the rules in gamified learning and education (Achterbosch, Miller, & Vamplew, 2017). The motive of the rule breaker is associated with the performance objectives. The rule breakers attempt to find an efficient way to achieve the performance objectives. They do not necessarily care if the "efficient way" is a right way, an expedient way, or a bad interpretation of the rules. They focus on achieving their goals with less effort. Some use the rule breaking as a way to show other students their abilities.

The behavioral characteristics of the rule breakers are associated with the "playful experiences" of competition, control, discovery, and subversion in the PLEX framework.

- Competition: Rule breakers try to achieve the performance objectives and be a successful competitor by any means necessary.
- Control: They make the bad use of the rules for controlling the situations in the gamified learning and education. Some of them feel superior to the other students from the control.
- Discovery: They look into the rules that their teacher announced to discover any weakness that can be used for achieving their goals.
- Subversion: They enjoy subverting the system of the gamified learning and education by breaking the rules in the class.

Information technology is not always necessary for gamifying learning and education, although it is helpful in the monitoring of student behavior. Technologies such as mobile apps, databases, or networks can provide teachers with tools to help keep negative experiences to a minimum. Teachers can implement gamification with cardboard, pencils, or stickers as well, however, when gamification does not use information technologies that monitor students' behaviors, the rule breakers tend to be more active and frequent. In these cases, teachers should make a concerted effort to reduce the impact of the rule breakers.

References

Achterbosch, L., Miller, C., & Vamplew, P. (2017). A taxonomy of griefer type by motivation in massively multiplayer online role-playing games. *Behaviour & Information Technology*. doi:10.1080/0144929X.2017.1306109

Bartle, R. (2005). Virtual worlds: Why people play. *Massively Multiplayer Game Development*, *2*, 1–16.

Berk, L. E. (2011). *Infants, children, and adolescents* (7th ed.). Boston, MA: Pearson Education.

Broidy, L. M., Nagin, D. S., Tremblay, R. E., Bates, J. E., Brame, B., Dodge, K. A., ... Vitaro, F. (2003). Developmental trajectories of childhood disruptive behaviors and adolescent delinquency: A six-site, cross-national study. *Developmental Psychology*, *39*(2), 222–245.

Davies, M. (2006, June 14). Gamers don't want any more grief. *The Guardian*. Retrieved from https://www.theguardian.com/

Edge. (2013). A history of griefing: Meet the gamers who, if you're lucky, only want to ruin your day for kicks. *EdgeOnline*. Retrieved from http://www.gamesradar.com/edge/

Kim, S. (2013). Analysis of engineering students' needs for gamification. *Journal on Knowledge and Data Engineering, 1*(1), 1–7.

Korhonen, H., Montola, M., & Arrasvunori, J. (2009). Understanding playful user experience through digital games. In A. Guenand (Ed.), *Proceedings of the 4th International Conference on Designing Pleasurable Products and Interfaces, DPPI 2009* (pp. 274–285). Compiègne, France: ACM Press.

Ladanyi, J., & Doyle-Portillo, S. (2017). The development and validation of the grief play scale (GPS) in MMORPGs. *Personality and Individual Differences, 114*, 125–133.

Lepper, M. R. (1988). Motivational considerations in the study of instruction. *Cognition and Instruction, 5*(4), 289–309.

Lin, H., & Sun, C. (2005, June 16–20). *The white-eyed player culture: grief play and construction of deviance in MMORPGs*. Paper presented at the Digital Games Research Association Conference (DIGRA) 2005, Vancouver, British Columbia, Canada. Retrieved from http://www.digra.org/digital-library/publications/the-white-eyed-player-culture-grief-play-and-construction-of-deviance-in-mmorpgs/

Malone, T. W. (1981). Toward a theory of intrinsically motivating instruction. *Cognitive Science, 5*(4), 333–369. doi:10.1016/S0364-0213(81)80017-1

Victoria, S. (2011). Griefing. *KnowYourMeme*. Retrieved from http://knowyourmeme.com/

Woolfolk, A. (2006). *Educational psychology* (10th ed.). Boston, MA: Allyn & Bacon.

Chapter 7
Gamification Framework

Quest

Let's try to understand the gamification framework.
Let's think of the role of the story for gamification.
Let's see the use for mechanics and how the mechanics can be used in games.
Let's try to understand the technologies for gamification and how they can be used in education and learning.

7.1 Gamification Framework for Education and Learning

There exist different views on the framework for games and gamification. This chapter begins with the introduction to gamification frameworks and elements for games. Hunicke, LeBlanc, and Zubek (2004) and Zichermann and Cunningham (2011) have suggested a theoretical gamification framework, which is the MDA framework, consisting of mechanics, dynamics, and aesthetics (see Fig. 7.1).

Mechanics are the components implemented for a game. With data and algorithms, mechanics define the behaviors allowed to the gamer and the control mechanisms of the game. In Monopoly, for example, the mechanics include dice, mortgage, title deed, and jail.

Dynamics define the interactions with the mechanics. It is the observable behaviors that gamers enact while playing a game. Taking ownership of a property can be one of the dynamics in Monopoly. Forming an alliance can be a good example of the dynamics in real-time strategy games or multiplayer online battle games.

Aesthetics describes the feeling and emotions that the gamer can experience from playing a game. It is the emotional response that game designers try to create in the gamers. It can be created by mechanics and dynamics. Sensation, fantasy, narrative, challenge, fellowship, discovery, expression, and submission can be the examples of aesthetics (Hunicke et al., 2004).

S. Kim et al., *Gamification in Learning and Education*, Advances in Game-Based Learning, DOI 10.1007/978-3-319-47283-6_7

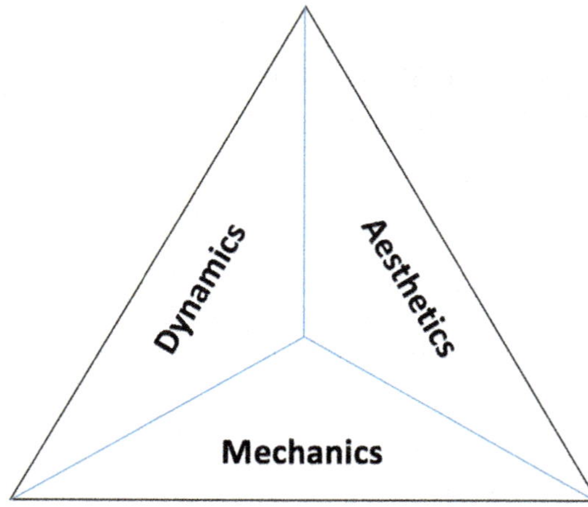

Fig. 7.1 MDA framework

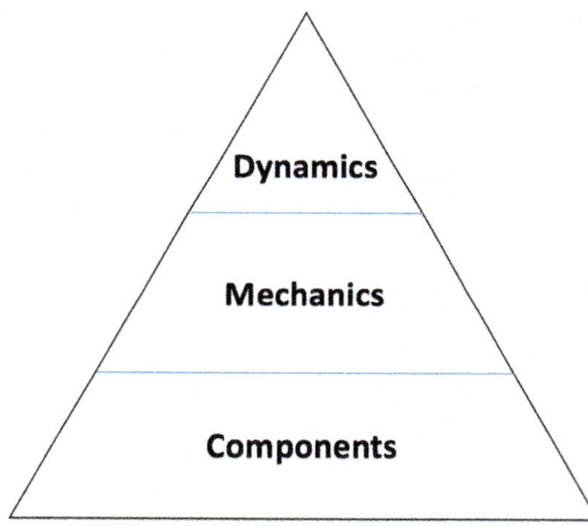

Fig. 7.2 Werbach and Hunter's gamification framework

Another view on the gamification framework has been proposed by Werbach and Hunter (2012). The researchers classified the gamification elements into dynamics, mechanics, and components (see Fig. 7.2).

Dynamics is the most abstract concept and biggest picture in a game or gamified system. It can be defined as the goals and objectives of an organization. Dynamics is comprised of five elements: constraints, emotions, narrative, progression, and relationships.

Mechanics are necessary for implementing dynamics in a game. It is the element that promotes gamers to engage in the game and behave as planned by game designers. Mechanics is comprised of ten elements: challenges, chances, competition, cooperation, feedback, resource acquisition, rewards, transactions, turns, and win states.

Components are the substantiated form of dynamics and mechanics, the least abstract element, and the closest element to the actual game or gamified system. There are 15 gamification components: achievements, avatars, badges, boss fights,

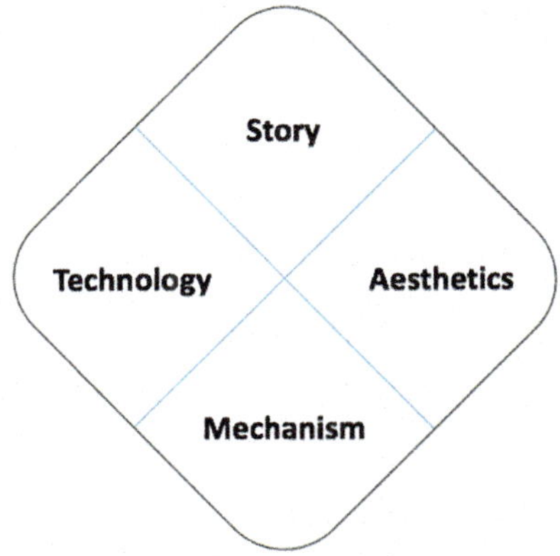

Fig. 7.3 Schell's gamification framework

collections, combat, content unlocking, gifting, leaderboards, levels, points, quests, social graphs, teams, and virtual goods.

The gamification framework of Bunchball (2016) is simpler than the other frameworks we have talked about so far. In the framework of Bunchball (2016), there are two elements: dynamics and mechanics. Bunchball (2016) defined *dynamics* as a gamer's experience attained through a game and *mechanics* as gamification elements required for providing gamers with the experience. Dynamics includes reward, status, achievement, self-expression, competition, and altruism. Mechanics includes points, levels, challenges, virtual goods and spaces, leaderboards, gift, and charity.

Schell (2014) defined four game elements: story, mechanism, technology, and aesthetics (see Fig. 7.3).

Story is a course of events that gamers can experience while playing a game. The story in a game can be developed in a linear structure or a branching structure. Story can be effectively delivered by the aesthetics and technology.

Mechanism describes the rules and procedures for a game. It defines the gamers' behaviors, rewards, and penalties in a game. The rewards and penalties affect the development of a story. There is no mechanism in novels, movies, and dramas since readers or audience cannot intervene in the story development.

Technology means situations, materials, and hardware required for creating a game. Many games employ information technologies. The technology, however, can also be a sheet of paper, a pencil, a Monopoly token, or other objects that we can see in our daily lives.

Aesthetics decides the look and feel that gamers can perceive within a game by audio and visual elements. Aesthetics directly influences gamers' experiences. Gamers can have a different experience from the stories that have different aesthetics, but the same story and mechanism.

There are some differences between terminologies in research, but the meanings of the terminologies are similar between research. This book employs an integrative gamification framework based on the research reviewed in this chapter (see Fig. 7.4).

Story provides a pivotal process leading an educational program. It consists of educational objectives and stories related to the objectives. Story can be divided into

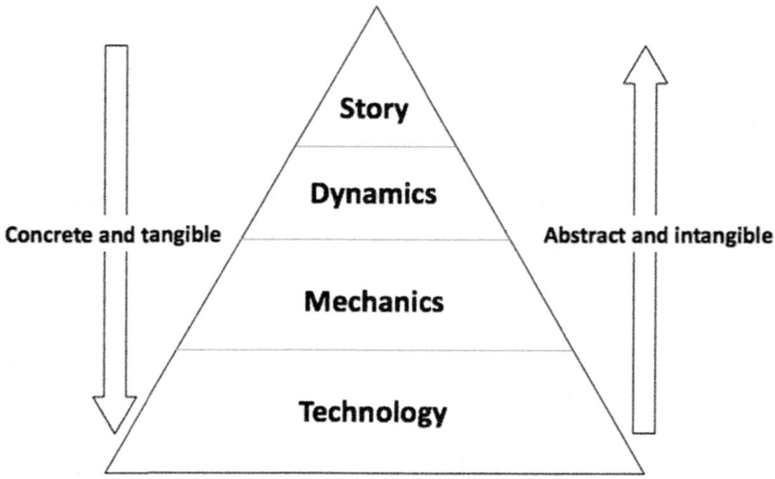

Fig. 7.4 Integrative gamification framework

various fun aspects. Dynamics, consisting of 20 fun experiences of PLEX, gives learners fun derived from the story. The purpose of the dynamics is to motivate learners to engage in learning. Mechanics implement dynamics at the level of data and algorithms. There are elements that learners can directly recognize in a game or gamified system. Learners receive feedback and rewards through the mechanics. Leaderboards, points, and badges are good examples of mechanics. Technology makes mechanics tangible and visible to learners. Learners can interact with a game or gamified system through technology. Technology in gamification includes hardware, software, network, and other objects.

7.2 Story

Most games intrinsically include stories. The story in gamification is not much different from one in novels, movies, or dramas. A difference is that gamers can intervene in and interact with a game, but the other genres do not allow audience to make changes in the development of a story. A gamer can decide if he or she will be a good entrepreneur or a greedy businessman in a game. While playing a game, gamers are exposed to a variety of options that require them to select a specific option to make progress in the game. Depending on the decision, a gamer can proceed to different story branches even though the gamers are all playing the same game.

Story strengthens the level of immersion and provides adventures and fantasy that people cannot experience in their daily lives. Story plays a role of the center axis that integrates fun experiences in a game. Gamers can experience adventure, competition, discovery, or other kinds of fun aspects planned and arranged to support the story in a game. Because of the story, gamers may continue thinking they are playing the game even when they are taking rest.

7.2.1 Origin of Story

Some games use stories that are developed specifically for the game, some adopt existing stories or modified versions of them. People may be familiar with the novel, *Gulliver's Travels* (Swift, 1726). A part of the novel talks about Laputa, which is an island floating in the sky. Laputa is made of advanced technologies. Grandville illustrated Laputa in 1856 (see Fig. 7.5).

Laputa appears again in the animated motion picture, *Castle in the Sky* (Takahata & Miyazaki, 1986). The Laputa image in the animation looks similar to the illustration in *Gulliver's Travels* (Swift, 1726). The appearance of Laputa does not stop here. Laputa turns up again in the Nintendo game, *Legend of Zelda: Skyward Sword* (Aonuma & Fujibayashi, 2011). Gamers in this game visit islands in the sky and solve problems that the residents on the islands have. There are shops selling equipment including bows and shields on the islands. Gamers can see forests, volcanos, deserts, or other backgrounds of the place. The names of the islands in this game are

Fig. 7.5 Laputa in Gulliver's Travels illustrated by J. J. Grandville (Reprinted from Wikimedia Commons, retrieved from https://commons.wikimedia.org)

not Laputa, but gamers who have read *Gulliver's Travels* (Swift, 1726) or watched *Castle in the Sky* (Takahata & Miyazaki, 1986) most likely notice the similarities.

The story of the video game *Transformers* (Hayasaka & Matsumoto, 2003) came from a cartoon. The *Transformers* (Bonaventura, Bryce, DeSanto, Murphy, & Bay, 2007) movie series and the game were all based on the cartoon series storyline. Contrary to the *Legend of Zelda* (Aonuma & Fujibayashi, 2011), the *Transformers* movie used the story of the game produced by Core Design in 1996.

7.2.2 Principle Rules of Storylining

The stories of many movies, dramas, and games have been derived from the adventures and journeys of the stories' heroes. Vogler and Montez (2007) suggest the 12-stage Hero's Journey model in their book "The Writer's Journey."

Stage 1. Ordinary world
Stage 2. Call to adventure
Stage 3. Refusal of the call
Stage 4. Meeting with the mentor
Stage 5. Crossing the first threshold
Stage 6. Tests, allies, enemies
Stage 7. Approach to the inmost cave
Stage 8. Ordeal
Stage 9. Reward (seizing the sword)
Stage 10. The road back
Stage 11. Resurrection
Stage 12. Return with the elixir

There are many novels, movies, dramas, and games that have used Vogler and Montez's (2007) model. Of course, not all stories include the 12 stages. Some stories have some of the stages in the model or sequence them differently.

Stories in gamification for education and learning are usually simpler than the 12-stage Hero's Journey model. In gamification of education and learning, it is more important to deliver meaningful knowledge than fun itself. That is, the role of the story in this context is to support education and learning, rather than to only create fun and entertainment as in novels, movies, dramas, or games.

7.3 Dynamics

Korhonen, Montola, and Arrasvunori (2009) suggested the Playful Experience framework (PLEX framework) for gamification dynamics. The PLEX framework consists of 20 categories of playful experiences. The following are the categories and the definition of each of them.

- Captivation: Experience of forgetting one's surroundings
- Challenge: Experience of having to develop and exercise skills in a challenging situation
- Competition: Experience of victory-oriented competition against oneself, opponent, or system
- Completion: Experience of completion, finishing, and closure, in relation to an earlier task or tension
- Control: Experience power, mastery, control, or virtuosity
- Discovery: Experience of discovering a new solution, place, or property
- Eroticism: Experience of sexual pleasure or arousal
- Exploration: Experience of exploring or investigating a world, affordance, puzzle, or situation
- Expression: Experience of creating something or expressing oneself in a creative fashion
- Fantasy: Experience of make-believe involving fantastical narratives, worlds, or characters
- Fellowship: Experience of friendship, fellowship, communality, or intimacy
- Nurture: Experience of nurturing, grooming, or caretaking
- Relaxation: Experience of unwinding, relaxation or stress relief, calmness during play
- Sadism: Experience of destruction and exerting power over others
- Sensation: Meaningful sensory experience
- Simulation: Experience of perceiving a representation of everyday life
- Subversion: Experience of breaking social roles, rules, and norms
- Suffering: Experience of frustration, anger, boredom, and disappointment typical to playing
- Sympathy: Experience of sharing emotional feelings
- Thrill: Experience of thrill derived from an actual or perceived danger or risk.

7.4 Mechanics

Schonfeld (2010) suggested a gamification mechanic based on a deck of cards developed for SCVNGR, a mobile gaming platform in which gamers visit places and perform activities to earn points. Table 7.1 shows the card deck for SCVNGR.

Kumar and Herger (2013), Duggan and Shoup (2013), Werbach and Hunter (2012), Zichermann and Linder (2013), and Bunchball (2016) all suggested different perspectives on mechanics. Leaderboard, however, is a common mechanic across the different perspectives. The badge, challenge (or quest), level, point, and virtual item (or good) are other common mechanics. Table 7.2 compares the gamification mechanics from research.

Table 7.3 shows the mechanic elements that are based on studies from Duggan and Shoup (2013), Kapp (2012), Kumar and Herger (2013), Radoff (2011), Schell (2014), and Zichermann and Linder (2013).

Table 7.1 Card Deck for SCVNGR

Achievement	Loyalty
Appointment dynamic	Meta game
Avoidance	Micro leaderboards
Behavioral contrast	Modifiers
Behavioral momentum	Moral hazard of game play
Blissful productivity	Ownership
Cascading information theory	Pride
Chain schedules	Privacy
Communal discovery	Progression dynamic
Companion gaming	Ratio reward schedules
Contingency	Real-time vs. delayed mechanics
Countdown	Reinforcer
Cross-situational leaderboard	Response
Disincentives	Reward schedules
Endless games	Rolling physical goods
Envy	Shell game
Epic meaning	Social fabric of games
Extinction	Status
Fixed interval reward schedules	Urgent optimism
Fixed ratio reward schedule	Variable interval reward schedules
Free lunch	Variable ratio reward schedule
Fun once, fun always	Viral game mechanics
Internal reward schedules	Virtual items
Lottery	

7.4.1 Rewards

- Point: Numerical reward for specific behaviors. Gamers can attain higher levels and receive badges by achieving target points (Experience points). In some cases, gamers can use the points for purchasing virtual goods or physical goods (Redeemable points). Also, gamers can give points to a gamer for his/her good behaviors or contributions (Karma points). The Karma points can facilitate altruism among gamers. Figure 7.6 illustrates a scene of SimCity BuildIt (Electronic Arts Inc., 2013) game, produced by Electronic Arts Inc. In this game, population size is a point. Players can achieve higher levels by increasing the population size.
- Level: Section of a game. Gamers can experience higher levels by completing a specific task. Some games use numbers to present different levels, but others use words. For example, peasants, merchants, farmers, knights, nobles, and monarch can be used for the levels in a game that has the medieval Europe as its setting. There can be a single level system or multiple level systems in a game. For example, physical strength, wisdom, and popularity levels can be simultaneously used for a game. Higher levels usually require gamers to complete more difficult tasks than lower levels do. The rewards are often bigger or

Table 7.2 Comparison of mechanics

Mechanics	S	K&H	D&S	W&H	Z&L	B
Achievement	Y			Y		
Appointment dynamic	Y					
Avatar				Y		
Avoidance	Y					
Badge		Y		Y	Y	
Behavioral contrast	Y					
Behavioral momentum	Y					
Blissful productivity	Y					
Boss fight				Y		
Cascading information theory	Y					
Chain schedules	Y					
Challenge & quest		Y	Y	Y		Y
Collection				Y		
Combat				Y		
Communal discovery	Y					
Companion gaming	Y					
Content unlocking				Y		
Contingency	Y					
Countdown	Y					
Cross-situational leaderboard	Y	Y	Y	Y	Y	Y
Disincentives	Y					
Emotion		Y				
Endless games	Y					
Envy	Y					
Epic meaning	Y					
Extinction	Y					
Feedback			Y			
Fixed interval reward schedules	Y				Y	
Fixed ratio reward schedule	Y				Y	
Free lunch	Y					
Fun once, fun always	Y					
Gifting & charity				Y		Y
Internal reward schedules	Y				Y	
Journey		Y				
Level			Y	Y	Y	Y
Lottery	Y					
Loyalty	Y					
Meta game	Y					
Micro leaderboards	Y	Y	Y	Y	Y	Y
Modifiers	Y					
Moral hazard of game play	Y					
Narrative		Y				

(continued)

Table 7.2 (continued)

Mechanics	S	K&H	D&S	W&H	Z&L	B
Onboarding		Y				
Ownership	Y					
Point		Y	Y	Y	Y	Y
Pride	Y					
Privacy	Y					
Progression dynamic	Y	Y				
Ratio reward schedules	Y				Y	
Real-time vs. delayed mechanics	Y					
Reinforcer	Y					
Relationship		Y				
Response	Y					
Reward schedules	Y				Y	
Rolling physical goods	Y					
Scaffolding		Y				
Shell game	Y					
Social fabric of games	Y					
Social graph				Y		
Status	Y					
Team				Y		
Urgent optimism	Y	Y				
Variable interval reward schedules	Y				Y	
Variable ratio reward schedule	Y				Y	
Viral game mechanics	Y					
Virtual items	Y			Y		Y

Table 7.3 Mechanic elements

Categories	Mechanics
Rewards	Point, level, progression, badge, authority, virtual good, physical good, discontinuation, gifting, free lunch, and virtual currency
Reward schedules	Fixed interval reward schedule, fixed ratio reward schedule, variable interval reward schedule, and variable ratio reward schedule
Avoidance	Discouragement and leaky bucket
Leaderboard	Macro leaderboard, micro leaderboard, indirect competition, and direct competition
Status	Avatar and social network
Quest	Unlocking content, countdown, lottery, communal discovery, and scaffolding

better at higher levels. However, the rate of increase in rewards is slower than the rate of increase in requirements necessary to advance to the next level. Thus, even though the game may progress at a slower pace, gamers feel that they receive more and better rewards. In Fig. 7.6, the number 44 on the top left side is the level.

Fig. 7.6 Population size as a point in SimCity BuildIt (Reproduced from SimCity BuildIt, Copyright 2013 by Electronic Arts Inc.)

- Progression: Means to show the degree of advancement in a game or sometimes within a level. Numbers, bar charts, line charts, pie charts, or images can be used for showing the progression. Some games mix these media. For example, a combination of a number and a pie chart can be used together to show a player's progress. SimCity BuildIt (Electronic Arts Inc., 2013) uses an image consisted of a number and a pie chart (see Fig. 7.6).
- Badge: Most visible achievement note. Badges can show other gamers the skills or accomplishment of a gamer. Gamers can win badges for completing necessary tasks. Some games use the badge as the level system and some others use the badge as a different mechanic. However, the badge usually does not have a fixed order and multiple badges are simultaneously used in a game. Because a badge is the mark showing the gamer who accomplished the same task, gamers can have a group identification by the badge (Antin & Churchill, 2011). Gamers collaborate more with other gamers in a group based on the group identification (Dawes, Van De Kragt, & Orbell, 1988). Figure 7.7 describes platinum keys in SimCity BuildIt (Electronic Arts Inc., 2013) game. In the game, a player can receive a platinum key when the player wins the Contest of Mayors. As a badge, the platinum key shows the player's achievement (see Fig. 7.7).

Fig. 7.7 Platinum keys as a badge in SimCity BuildIt (Reproduced from SimCity BuildIt, Copyright 2013 by Electronic Arts Inc.)

- Authority: Capacity or ability to control game elements and gamers. When a gamer achieves a specific level, the gamer can be authorized to control characters, shops, villages, or other gamers. The authority can be limited by the specific time period, the number of times used, or the associated event. Some games give gamers unlimited authority. Figures 7.8 and 7.9 illustrate NeoBank and OMEGA storage in SimCity BuildIt (Electronic Arts Inc., 2013) game. Not all players can have these buildings. Only those who achieve a specific level can build and use these buildings.
- Virtual Goods: Goods that can be attained, purchased, or traded within a game. Most representative virtual goods are clothes, accessories, and weapons. Gamers can increase the game speed, make the game character stronger, and unlock special content by the virtual goods. Figure 7.10 shows factories and shops that produce virtual goods, such as wood, steel, hammers, or donuts. Players can sell or purchase the virtual goods through a trade depot. Some games allow a player to decide the price of each good. Through such experience, the player can understand the market, pricing strategy, and customer behaviors. Figure 7.11 illustrates a trade depot in which players sell or purchase virtual goods.
- Physical Goods: Goods that have value in a real world. Gamers can attain the physical goods by an achievement in the game or the use of virtual goods. Some games give gamers real money based on the gamer's achievement. Some people may not believe that there is a game item that can be sold at about $45,000. Lineage is a massively multiplayer online role-playing game. The players in this game need better weapons to achieve higher goals. They can make the weapon

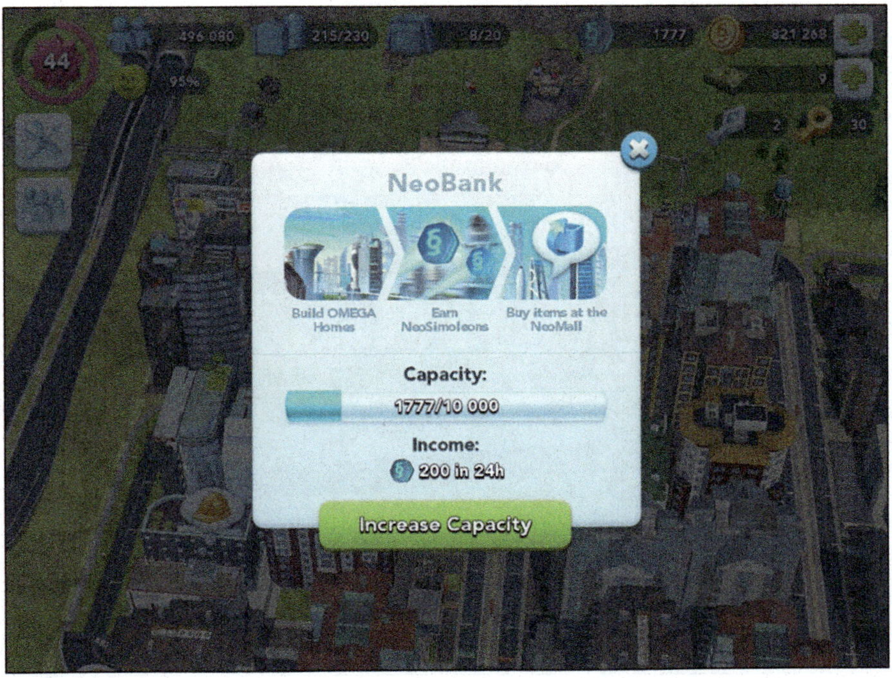

Fig. 7.8 NeoBank in SimCity BuildIt (Reproduced from SimCity BuildIt, Copyright 2013 by Electronic Arts Inc.)

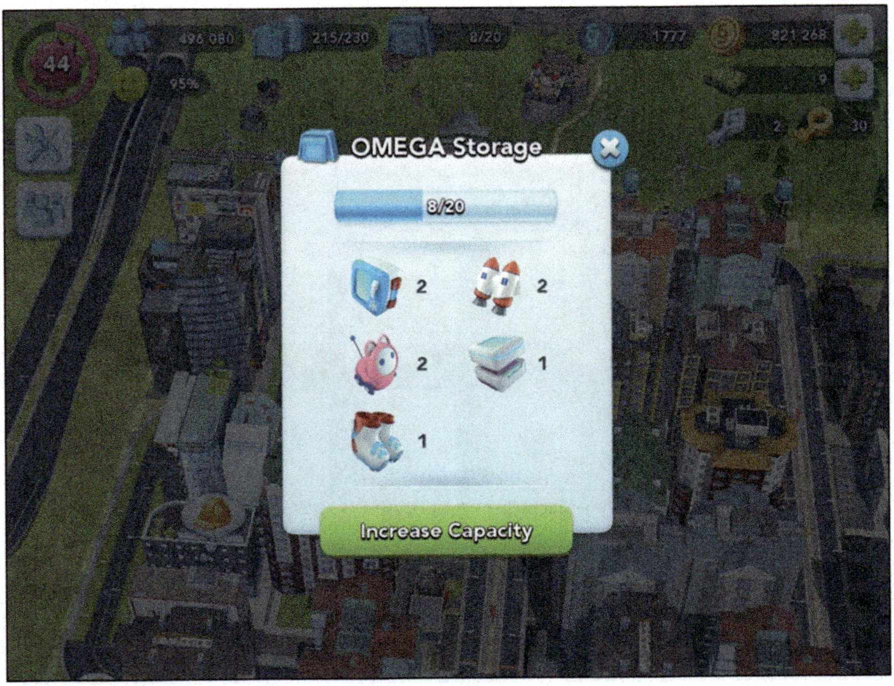

Fig. 7.9 OMEGA storage in SimCity BuildIt (Reproduced from SimCity BuildIt, Copyright 2013 by Electronic Arts Inc.)

Fig. 7.10 Producing virtual goods in SimCity BuildIt (Reproduced from SimCity BuildIt, Copyright 2013 by Electronic Arts Inc.)

Fig. 7.11 Trading virtual goods in SimCity BuildIt (Reproduced from SimCity BuildIt, Copyright 2013 by Electronic Arts Inc.)

within the game, but some of them want to have the weapon without investing much time. Because of this reason, they pay real money to buy virtual goods from other players.
- Discontinuation: Device to limit the reward according to a specific behavior. Some gamers repeat a behavior for attaining more rewards. Discontinuation can prevent this kind of behavior.
- Gifting: Giving other gamers the items. Gamers can buy a gift for another player with Karma points. Also, gamers can give other gamers their items. Gifting can be more frequently observed in games that require an active team play to achieve higher goals.
- Free Lunch: Reward without own effort. Gamers sometimes can receive a reward regardless of achievements. The volume and quality of the free lunch can vary depending on the player's progress. Some free lunches disappear after a specific period of time. This mechanism encourages players to visit the game regularly. Some games use this mechanism to advertise their virtual goods to create revenue. Figure 7.12 shows a gift box as a free lunch in SimCity BuidIt (Electronic Arts Inc., 2013). The player in the game sometimes, not always, can see the gift box in the player's city or other players' cities.
- Virtual Currency: Currency that has value only within a game. Gamers can use the virtual currency for purchasing or selling items. Gamers can attain virtual currency by achievement in a game or paying with real money. Figures 7.13 and 7.14 illustrate two kinds of virtual currencies in SimCity BuildIt (Electronic Arts Inc.,

Fig. 7.12 A gift box as a free lunch in SimCity BuildIt (Reproduced from SimCity BuildIt, Copyright 2013 by Electronic Arts Inc.)

Fig. 7.13 Simoleons in SimCity BuildIt (Reproduced from SimCity BuildIt, Copyright 2013 by Electronic Arts Inc.)

Fig. 7.14 SimCash in SimCity BuildIt (Reproduced from SimCity BuildIt, Copyright 2013 by Electronic Arts Inc.)

2013). Simoleons in Fig. 7.13 is the main virtual currency that can be earned by making the city larger and the citizens happy. The player in the game can use Simoleons to build or upgrade buildings, develop land, and purchase necessary virtual goods. Meanwhile, SimCash in Fig. 7.14 is a more valuable virtual currency. It is hard to earn and can be used for significantly improving the speed of game progress. As a result, some players who want to upgrade their cities as soon as possible pay money for SimCash. Like SimCity BuildIt (Electronic Arts Inc., 2013), some games use multiple virtual currencies to create more revenue, as well as engage more players.

7.4.2 Reward Schedules: Algorithms for Rewards

- Fixed Interval Reward Schedule: Rewards are provided to a player on a specific time schedule. For example, the stamina of a game character increases by 1 stamina point every 3 min.
- Fixed Ratio Reward Schedule: Rewards are provided when a gamer completes a defined number of missions. For example, the stamina of a game character increase 3 stamina points after consuming an energy beverage.
- Variable Interval Reward Schedule: Rewards are provided at irregular time intervals. Unlike fixed interval reward schedules, gamers can receive a reward at various time intervals.
- Variable Ratio Reward Schedule: Rewards are provided when a gamer completes a mission, but the number or difficulty of missions is different each time. For example, a gamer needs to catch ten monsters to receive the reward; then later, the gamer needs to catch 20 monsters instead.

7.4.3 Avoidance: Behavior to Avoid Penalties

- Discouragement: A penalty given when a gamer does not avoid a specific behavior. Discouragement is for preventing gamers from demonstrating a specific behavior. It is the opposite of the reward concept.
- Leaky Bucket: Limitation given over time. Gamers can perform a quest without any limitation at the beginning of the game, but they face limitation over time (Duggan & Shoup, 2013). The limitation can be implemented by the maximum number of available quests or the duration of a quest. For example, in the quest of filling up a leaky bucket, let's assume that gamers can fill up the bucket by pouring water in it ten times. However, 10% of the water inside the bucket disappears every 12 min. As a result, gamers can fill up the leaky bucket once every 12 min after they fill up the bucket. The leaky bucket mechanics can be found in the Hay Day (Supercell, 2012), a mobile farming game. Gamers can experience the leaky bucket when they bake bread. Gamers may use virtual goods to reduce the time for baking.

7.4.4 Leaderboard: A Board Showing Leading Gamers' Achievements.

- Macro Leaderboard: A board showing the names, rankings, and scores of the gamers leading the overall game. During the game, the macro leaderboard shows the interim score or ranking of the gamers. When the game ends, it shows the final score or ranking of the gamers. The macro leaderboard in Hay Day (Supercell, 2012) shows the rankings, names, and scores of the gamers loading goods on a freight vessel.
- Micro Leaderboard: A board showing the names, rankings, and scores of the gamers leading the game within a region or a level. The structure of the micro leaderboard is similar to the macro leaderboard. The micro leaderboard encourages beginner or intermediate gamers to compete with others for reward since they compete only with the gamers limited by a region or level. They do not need to worry about competitors that are too strong to compete against. Figure 7.15 illustrates a micro leaderboard in SimCity BuildIt (Electronic Arts Inc., 2013). Depending on the game progress, a player belongs to a league and competes with other players who are in the same league.
- Indirect Competition: Competition based on relative progression of the game. Gamers do not need to compete with other gamers in the indirect competition. That is, one gamer's progression or achievement does not affect other gamers'

Fig. 7.15 A micro leaderboard in SimCity BuildIt (Reproduced from SimCity BuildIt, Copyright 2013 by Electronic Arts Inc.)

rankings. This type of competition is appropriate for the networker and the friend types. Figure 7.16 shows an indirect competition in SimCity BuildIt (Electronic Arts Inc., 2013). In Figure 7.16, the player needs to complete three tasks to develop a beach area. The successful completion of the tasks influences only that player's progress.

- Direct Competition: Competition between players. If a player achieves more than other players do, the player's ranking goes up and the other players' rankings go down. Figure 7.17 shows a direct competition in SimCity BuildIt (Electronic Arts Inc., 2013). A player has to compete with other players to win the Contest of Mayors.

7.4.5 Status: Avatar, Ranking, or Social Relationship Within a Game

- Avatar: An avatar visually describes the gamer. A player can use an abstract image as well as a picture of the player. An avatar sometimes embeds its ability or characteristic. With an avatar, as a result, other players can see a player's ability or characteristic without looking into the player's profile. Some games sell accessories that can be used for adorning the avatar. Since some accessories improve the ability of avatars, some players purchase them.

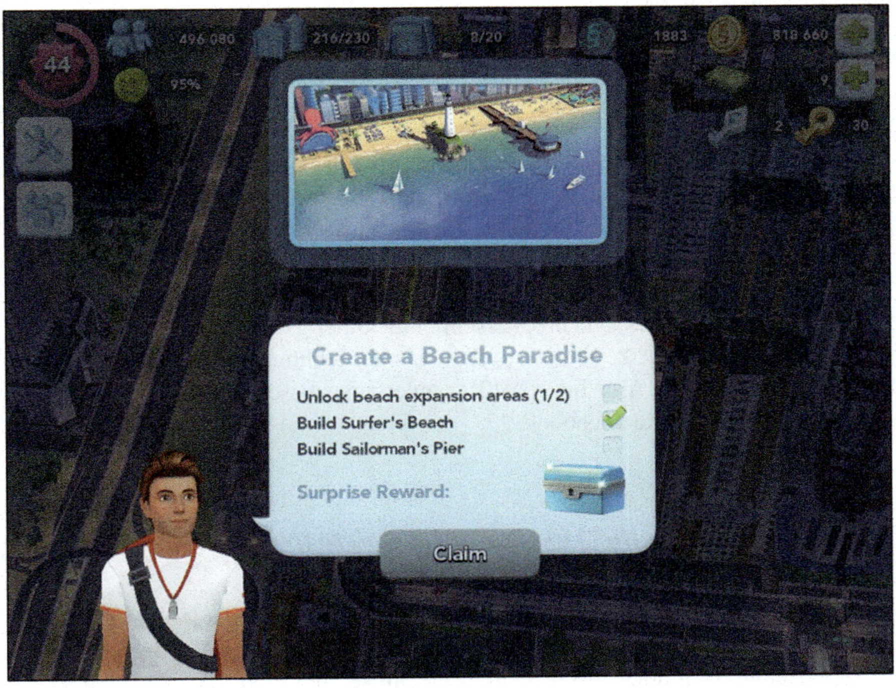

Fig. 7.16 An indirect competition in SimCity BuildIt (Reproduced from SimCity BuildIt, Copyright 2013 by Electronic Arts Inc.)

Fig. 7.17 A direct competition in SimCity BuildIt (Reproduced from SimCity BuildIt, Copyright 2013 by Electronic Arts Inc.)

- Ranking: Ranking is a result of competition with other players. While points and levels can be affected by a player's achievements, ranking can be also influenced by other players' achievements. As with the two types of leaderboards, ranking can be also determined by overall achievements within a whole game or an achievement category. Ranking is a criterion for rewards as well as a result of a player's achievements. High rankers are usually more interested in their rankings than low rankers are.
- Social Network: Social networks show the status of other gamers. The gamer can see the names, avatars, and progression of the other gamers. The gamer can click "Recommend" or "Like" button to share his/her feelings or thoughts. In SimCity BuildIt (Electronic Arts Inc., 2013), gamers can be connected through social network services like Facebook.

7.4.6 *Quest: Specific Mission to Complete to Receive Rewards*

- Unlocking Content: Gamers cannot experience the locked content unless they complete a specific quest or reach a required level or point. If gamers meet the requirement to unlock the content, they can see the items, scenes, characters, functions, or missions that they could not see before unlocking the content.

- Countdown: Given time to complete a specific quest. Gamers need to complete a specific quest or perform a behavior within the given time.
- Lottery: Reward type with haphazardness. Gamers can attain this type of reward by accident or for an unintended behavior.
- Communal Discovery: Quest completed by gamers' collaboration. A single gamer cannot complete this kind of mission. Communal discovery must be completed by gamers' collaboration.
- Scaffolding: Support for the gamers who need help to perform a quest. Scaffolding can be implemented by help message, agent/hasher, shared strategy, and so on. Figure 7.18 illustrates FAQ for the Contest of Mayors in SimCity BuildIt (Electronic Arts Inc., 2013). This FAQ is used as scaffolding for those who need help to participate in the contest.

7.5 Technology

Gamification for learning and education needs various technologies for implementation. Gamification can be implemented by not only information technologies, but also things in our real life such as paper, wooden sticks, badges, stickers, cards, or different types of toys. Though this book focuses on information technologies, the readers do not need to limit the range of technologies for gamification.

Fig. 7.18 FAQ as scaffolding in SimCity BuildIt (Reproduced from SimCity BuildIt, Copyright 2013 by Electronic Arts Inc.)

The technology in this book will be explained by two large categories: hardware and software.

7.5.1 Hardware

7.5.1.1 Wearable Devices

Many gamified learning and education users have used computers, tablets, and smartphones as a user device. With those devices, learners can participate in apps, websites, or social network services that employ gamification. These devices will serve the needs of gamification until existing technology enters a saturation phase and newer technology is developed to replace them.

Look back on the feature phone market in 2005 and 2006. The feature phone market was at the saturation state and a revolutionary device, iPhone, appeared in 2007. Technology S-Curve (Christensen, 1992; Foster, 1986; Scillitoe, 2013) explains the patterns observed in this situation. That is, a new product or service tends to come to the market when an existing product or service is at the saturation phase. Many market reports have shown the smartphone market is already at the saturation phase. This means a new product that can replace the smartphone will appear.

Most possible substitute goods are wearable devices, suggested by MIT (Massachusetts Institute of Technology) in 1966, meaning devices or computers that are worn on clothing or a part of human body. With a wearable device, a person can interact with the device by gaze, voice, or gesture. Some industries like clothing, textile, glasses, auto, and shipbuilding have been using wearable devices. The application of the wearable device can influence gamification in learning and education. In this section, some wearable devices will be reviewed to note their characteristics and potential utilization for gamification in learning and education.

Google Glass Google developed Google Glass which can be controlled by voice and a touchpad. The transparent glass of this device is used for displaying information. Although the glass is small, the user does not recognize its true size. Instead, the user experiences the feeling that it is a 25-inch monitor that is about 95 inches away. Though some issues exist such as price, privacy, and usability, Google Glass still has potential uses in gamification.

Jawbone's UP Jawbone has developed a series of wearable devices for healthcare, named UP. People can see the information on their sleep, activity, calories burned, and heart health by connecting UP to a smartphone. UP tracks the behavioral patterns of the user and provides advice to improve the user's health. These features of UP can be applied for physical training, medicine, or other industries, especially some tasks asking appropriate physical conditions of workers.

Sight Systems In 2012, Eran May-raz and Daniel Lazo shared a video on YouTube (May-raz & Daniel, 2012). The video was created to meet the graduation requirement of Bezalel Academy of Arts in Israel. They named the video Sight Systems and tried to show their audience a future in which people used wearable devices in their daily lives. Figure 7.19 is a screenshot of Sight Systems. The person in the video is performing a superman exercise. He is using a wearable device similar to contact lenses (see Fig. 7.20).

Using the wearable device, he can experience a virtual experience. Figure 7.21 shows what he can see during the superman exercise.

With the wearable device imagined in *Sight Systems*, people can experience gamified cooking. While they are cooking, they are asked to complete missions to achieve higher scores. The missions play a role of scaffolding or direct instruction for successful cooking. In Fig. 7.22, for example, there are dashed lines on a vegetable to show where the person should cut (May-raz & Lazo, 2012).

Figure 7.23 illustrates a scene that a player can see during gameplay. The left side of the screen shows a mission that the player has to complete to achieve a goal. If the wearable device recognizes that the player successfully completes this stage of the mission (tilting the pan to move the egg), the player can move forward to the next stage (May-raz & Lazo, 2012).

The wearable device in *Sight Systems* can be used for dating. While dating, the user is asked to complete certain quests that can make the dating successful. If the user completes the quests, the level of favorability represented in the score is increased (May-raz & Lazo, 2012) (see Fig. 7.24).

Fig. 7.19 Superman exercise using a wearable device (Reproduced from "Sight," by Robot Genius, 2012, retrieved from www.robotgeniusfilms.com Copyright 2012 by Robot Genius)

Fig. 7.20 A player's eyes with wearable devices (Reproduced from "Sight," by Robot Genius, 2012, retrieved from www.robotgeniusfilms.com Copyright 2012 by Robot Genius)

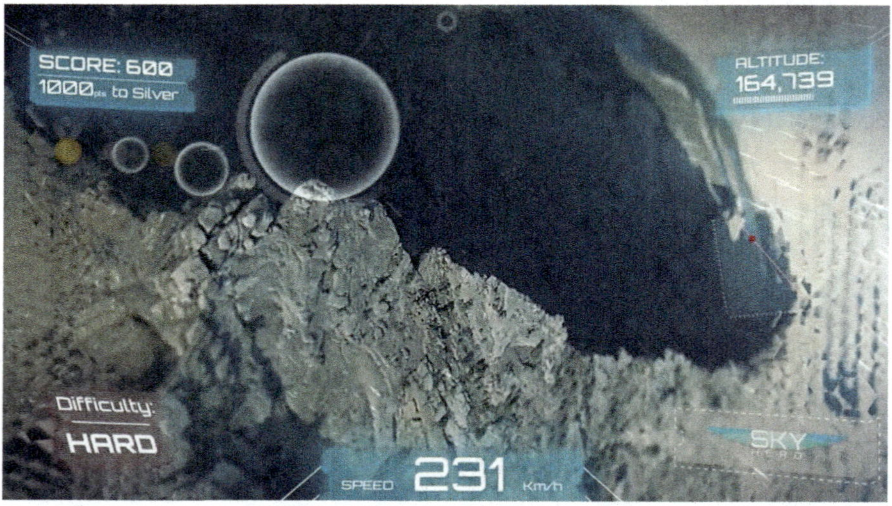

Fig. 7.21 A scene from the game for superman exercise (Reproduced from "Sight," by Robot Genius, 2012, retrieved from www.robotgeniusfilms.com Copyright 2012 by Robot Genius)

7.5.1.2 Augmented Reality

Augmented reality is a technology that makes the real-world environment more valuable or easy to use by adding meaningful information created by information technologies. For example, augmented reality can add navigation information for someone who is walking or driving on a new road (see Fig. 7.25).

Fig. 7.22 Gamified cooking using a wearable device (Reproduced from "Sight," by Robot Genius, 2012, retrieved from www.robotgeniusfilms.com Copyright 2012 by Robot Genius)

Fig. 7.23 A mission in gamified cooking (Reproduced from "Sight," by Robot Genius, 2012, retrieved from www.robotgeniusfilms.com Copyright 2012 by Robot Genius)

Another good example of the application of augmented reality is fixing vehicles at home. The user of Google Glass follows step-by-step instructions for diagnosing and fixing problems. Google Glass not only provides the instruction, but also detects if the user actually follows the instruction. From the visual information collected by the camera in Glass, it can decide if the user correctly followed the instruction.

Fig. 7.24 Dating using a wearable device (Reproduced from "Sight," by Robot Genius, 2012, retrieved from www.robotgeniusfilms.com Copyright 2012 by Robot Genius)

Fig. 7.25 Navigation information provided by Google Glass (Reproduced from Google Glass Youtube Channel, by Google, 2013, retrieved from https://www.youtube.com Copyright 2013 by Google)

7.5.2 Software

It is difficult to implement gamification for learning and education only with hardware technologies. Most hardware does not work without accompanying software. Radoff (2011) includes graphic design and programming in the technologies necessary for developing social games, which are hosted on social network services. However, this section focuses on the gamification platform and development tools rather than programming languages or graphic software.

7.5.2.1 Gamification Platform

A gamification platform tracks, measures, and logs gamers' behaviors within gamified learning and education. It gives gamers feedback and rewards based on their behaviors. For the developers and administrators, it provides the analysis tool and the programming library connected to legacy systems.

It is not always necessary to employ a gamification platform for developing gamified apps and websites. However, with the gamification platform, the development can be more convenient and efficient since the platform provides common development resources (Zhu, Pei, & Shang, 2017). Especially when developing large-scale gamification programs, the use of a gamification platform can reduce the development time, cost, and the risks associated with the major requirement change.

Herzig, Ameling, and Schill (2012) suggest a generic platform for enterprise gamification, which includes analytics, game data, business rule management system (BRMS), and game rules and mechanics. The platform can collect and analyze the data on users' behaviors with game data and analytics components. Also, designers and developers can control the gamification programs in the platform by manipulating the BRMS and game rules and mechanics.

The generic gamification platform is not integrated with legacy systems. As a result, it is more flexible than an integrated gamification solution since it does not need to meet the rules of the legacy systems, and it communicates with the legacy system through application program interface (API) which is a set of definitions of routine and subroutines, protocols, and libraries (Herzig, et al., 2012).

The generic gamification platform is more scalable than an integrated gamification solution since it supports multiple systems inside or outside organizations. A downside caused by its scalability is that it can be hard to ensure required performance levels in some situations. Thus, it may be an effective strategy to estimate possible performance before expanding the platform coverage (Herzig, et al., 2012).

Figure 7.26 illustrates an enterprise gamification platform that is based on the generic gamification platform suggested by Herzig et al. (2012). Unlike the generic platform, in the enterprise platform the communication channel is separated into two separate channels: internal and external channels. Because of security issues and system performance, most corporations separate the communication channel. The enterprise gamification platform in Fig. 7.26 reflects this practical practice. Users send and receive data to and from the gamification platform via an external communication channel. In addition, an internal communication channel is used for the interaction between the gamification platform and the legacy systems or the gamification administrator.

Herger (2011) suggests a checklist for evaluating gamification platforms, which consists of nine categories: game mechanics, functionality, programmability, security, administration, platform architecture, nonfunctional requirements, business model, and company profile. Table 7.4 shows the criteria in each category.

Kim (2014) suggests a decision-making framework for selecting a gamification platform. Table 7.5 illustrates the criteria for each category and subcategory.

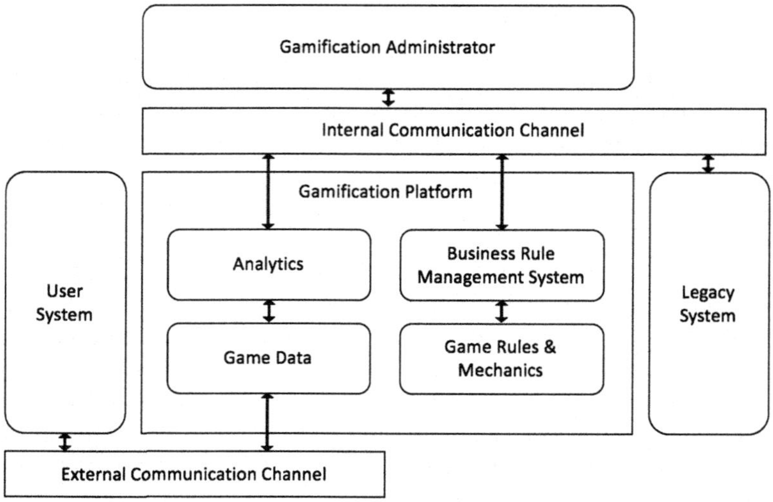

Fig. 7.26 An enterprise gamification platform based on generic gamification platform suggested by Herzig et al. (2012)

Table 7.4 Checklist for evaluating gamification platforms

Category	Criteria
Game mechanics	Rank/levels/achievements, currencies, measures, feedback, individual avatar, communication system, 3D environment, marketplace, economy, teams, time pressure, competition, difficulty adaption, learning path, fun failure, social connectivity, meaning/purpose
Functionality	Default currencies, default achievements/badges, distinction between currencies & measures, currency transactions, customizability of currencies/levels/badges/goods, customizability of goals/rules, repository for mechanics/missions/artifacts, goals & rules engine, transaction engine, data push, data location, integration with ERP system
Programmability	API access, API libraries, complexity, extension concept
Security	Confidentiality, integrity, availability, access control, data authenticity, player authenticity, single sign on
Administration	Analytics, separator of duties, administrator levels
Platform architecture	Infrastructure, databases, operating systems, scalability, delivery model, security, interoperability, backup/high availability
Nonfunctional requirements	Accessibility, documentation, localization, maintainability, open source, integration, response time, community
Business model	Licensing
Company profile	Development/support team structure, reference customers, roadmap/strategy

Bunchball is one of the gamification platform and solution vendors. Nitro (Bunchball, 2007) is a gamification platform that supports user engagement, loyalty management, sales promotion, customer retention, customer behavior change, employee motivation, and employee training (Hate, 2013).

Table 7.5 Decision criteria for selecting gamification platform

Category	Subcategory	Criteria
Credibility of supplier	Business record	Market share, sales history, and partnership
	Expertise	Number of gamification professionals, success story
Product competitiveness	Terms of sale	Price, marketing program
	Product architecture	Hardware requirements, supported operating systems, development languages, supported databases
	Features	Supported gamification mechanics, connectivity to external game engines, security, analytics
	Performance	Functionality, reliability, usability, efficiency, maintainability, portability
Service continuity	Stability of supplier	Financial stability, vision, and experience of executives
	Terms of contract	Terms of warranty, terms of product liability

There are many gamification platform and solution vendors including Badgeville, Behave.io, Beintoo, Bemore, BizPart Engage, Bunchball, Busification, CellCast Solution, CRMGamified, Echo.it, EMee, Freshdesk Arcade, Funifier, Gameboxed, GamEffective, Gametize, Gaminside, Gimmie, H Engage, Hoopla, Hooptap, Hopskoch, Influitive, Keas, LevelsPro, Pactify, ParWinr, PropsToYou, RedCritter Connecter, SAP Enterprise Gamification Platform, ShapeUp, Wheeldo, Wonnova, and Zurmo.

7.6 Tools for Developing Games and Augmented Reality

- Unity: Unity (Unity Technologies, 2004) is a game engine for developing 2D or 3D games. It supports multiple operating systems such as Windows, Mac OS X, Android, and iOS. It can also be used for developing games for video games like X-Box and PlayStation. The programming languages that Unity (Unity Technologies, 2004) supports are C#, Boo, and JavaScript. With this particular game engine, developers do not need to write codes for common functions supported by the engine. As a result, the speed of game development can be increased and the quality of outcomes can be assured. This can reduce developers' workloads related to graphic rendering, physical engine, network, geography, audio, video, and animation.
- GameMaker: GameMaker (Overmars, 1999) is a tool for people, with or without programming skills, to develop games. It uses graphic user interface and game developers can drag-and-drop instead of writing codes. It is a cross-platform tool and supports Windows, Mac OS X, Android, iOS, and PlayStation. Although GameMaker can be a useful tool for developing games because of its intuitive user interface, it is also limited to developing noncomplicated games.
- ARToolKit: ARToolKit (Kato, 1999) is an open-source programming library for developing applications using augmented reality. With ARToolKit using computer vision techniques, developers can easily overlay virtual objects.

ARToolKit supports smart glasses, GPS, compass, optical stereo calibration, and camera position and orientation tracking.

- FreshAir: FreshAir (Mogo Mobile Inc., 2014) is a development tool for implementing augmented reality based on geographic information. People can use the FreshAir Editor, which is a web-based editor, for developing augmented reality applications without any programming codes. FreshAir can be used for developing games, university tour, city guide, educational programs (Dunleavy, 2014).

The elements for gamification in learning and education are story, dynamics, mechanics, and technology. However, this does not mean that all of the four elements must be used for gamification in learning and education. Also, using many gamification elements does not ensure more effective gamification or better results (Mora, Riera, González, & Arnedo-Moreno, 2017). Considering the given conditions, educators should choose necessary gamification elements and make them as an integrated solution, no matter how large, to solve problems in learning and education.

Let's trace back our memory to when we were young children. Most of us were pleased with a "Great Job!" stamp that a teacher gave us. It encouraged us to deliver a better performance. Using the stamp, or a course with fair and clear reward rules, is a form of gamification. The quality of gamification in learning and education is not determined by the size of the gamification.

References

Antin, J., & Churchill, E. F. (2011, May). Badges in social media: A social psychological perspective. In *CHI 2011 Gamification Workshop Proceedings* (pp. 1–4). New York, NY: ACM.

Aonuma, E. (Producer), & Fujibayashi, H. (Director). (2011). *The Legend of Zelda*. Japan: Nintendo.

Bonaventura, L., Bryce, I., DeSanto, T., Murphy, D. (Producers), & Bay, M. (Director). (2007). *Transformers*. United States: Di Bonaventura Pictures.

Bunchball. (2007). *Nitro*. Available from https://www.bunchball.com/products/nitro/

Bunchball. (2016). *Gamification 101: An introduction to game dynamics* [White paper]. Retrieved January 24, 2017, from Bunchball.com

Christensen, C. M. (1992). Exploring the limits of the technology s-curve. Part I: Component technologies. *Production and Operations Management, 1*(4), 334–357. doi:10.1111/j.1937-5956.1992.tb00001.x

Dawes, R. M., Van De Kragt, A. J., & Orbell, J. M. (1988). Not me or thee but we: The importance of group identity in eliciting cooperation in dilemma situations: Experimental manipulations. *Acta Psychologica, 68*(1), 83–97.

Duggan, K., & Shoup, K. (2013). *Business gamification for dummies*. Hoboken, NJ: Wiley.

Dunleavy, M. (2014). Design principles for augmented reality learning. *TechTrends, 58*(1), 28–34.

Electronic Arts Inc. (2013). *SimCity BuildIt*. Available from https://www.ea.com/games/simcity/simcity-buildit

Foster, R. N. (1986). *Innovation: The attacker's advantage*. New York, NY: Summit Books.

Hate, S. (2013). Enterprise gamification architecture strategy. *Gamification: Rediscover the Power of Engagement, 11*(3), 55.

Hayasaka, N. (Producer), & Matsumoto, K. (Director). (2003). *Transformers*. Japan: Winkysoft.

Herger, M. (2011, October 24). *A checklist for evaluating gamification platforms*. Retrieved from http://www.enterprise-gamification.com/

Herzig, P., Ameling, M., & Schill, A. (2012, August 20–24). *A generic platform for enterprise gamification*. Paper presented at the 2012 Joint 10th Working IEEE/IFIP Conference on Software Architecture (WICSA) and 6th European Conference on Software Architecture (ECSA). Retrieved January 24, 2017, from IEEE Xplore. doi:10.1109/WICSA-ECSA.212.33

Hunicke, R., LeBlanc, M., & Zubek, R. (2004, July). MDA: A formal approach to game design and game research. In *Proceedings of the AAAI Workshop on Challenges in Game AI* (Vol. 4, No. 1). Retrieved from http://www.cs.northwestern.edu/~hunicke/MDA.pdf

Kapp, K. (2012). *The gamification of learning and instruction: Game-based methods and strategies for training and education*. San Francisco, CA: Pfeiffer.

Kato, H. (1999). *ARToolKit*. Available from https://artoolkit.org

Kim, S. (2014). Decision support model for introduction of gamification solution using AHP. *The Scientific World Journal, 2014*, 1–7.

Korhonen, H., Montola, M., & Arrasvunori, J. (2009). Understanding playful user experience through digital games. In A. Guenand (Ed.), *Proceedings of the 4th International Conference on Designing Pleasurable Products and Interfaces, DPPI 2009* (pp. 274–285). Compiègne, France: ACM Press.

Kumar, J., & Herger, M. (2013). *Gamification at work: Designing engaging business software*. Retrieved from https://www.interaction-design.org

May-raz, E., & Lazo, D. (2012). *Sight systems*. Israel: Robot Genius.

Mogo Mobile Inc. (2014). *FreshAir*. Available from http://www.playfreshair.com

Mora, A., Riera, D., González, C., & Arnedo-Moreno, J. (2017). Gamification: A systematic review of design frameworks. *Journal of Computing in Higher Education*. doi:10.1007/s12528-017-9150-4

Overmars, M. (1999). *GameMaker*. Available from https://www.yoyogames.com

Radoff, J. (2011). *Game on: Energize your business with social media games*. Indianapolis, IN: Wiley Publishing, Inc.

Schell, J. (2014). *The art of game design: A book of lenses* (2nd ed.). Boca Raton, FL: CRC Press.

Schonfeld, E. (2010, August 25). *SCVNGR's secret game mechanics playdeck*. Retrieved from https://techcrunch.com

Scillitoe, J. L. (2013). Technology S-curve. In E. H. Kessler (Ed.), *Encyclopedia of management theory* (Vol. 2, pp. 846–849). Thousand Oaks, CA: SAGE Reference. Retrieved from http://ezproxy.lib.vt.edu/login?url=http://go.galegroup.com.ezproxy.lib.vt.edu/ps/i.do?p=GVRL&sw=w&u=viva_vpi&v=2.1&it=r&id=GALE%7CCX3719100270&sid=summon&asid=67588320b3b844e91597dc092854603b

Supercell. (2012). *Hay Day*. Finland: Supercell.

Swift, J. (1726). *Gulliver's travels*. London, UK: Benjamin Motte.
Takahata, I. (Producer), & Miyazaki, H. (Director). (1986). *Castle in the Sky*. Japan: Studio Ghibli.
Unity Technologies. (2004). *Unity*. Available from https://unity3d.com
Vogler, C., & Montez, M. (2007). *The writer's journey: Mythic structure for writers* (3rd ed.). Studio City, CA: Michael Wiese Productions.
Werbach, K., & Hunter, D. (2012). *For the win: How game thinking can revolutionize your business*. Philadelphia, PA: Wharton Digital Press.
Zhu, Y., Pei, L., & Shang, J. (2017, June). Improving video engagement by gamification: A proposed design of MOOC videos. In S. Cheung, L. Kwok, W. Ma, L. K. Lee, & H. Yang (Eds.), *Proceedings of the International Conference on Blended Learning (ICBL) 2017* (pp. 433–444). Hong Kong, China: Springer.
Zichermann, G., & Cunningham, C. (2011). *Gamification by design: Implementing game mechanics in web and mobile apps*. Sebastopol, CA: O'Reilly Media.
Zichermann, G., & Linder, J. (2013). *The gamification revolution: How leaders leverage game mechanics to crush the competition*. New York, NY: Mc Graw Hill Education.

Chapter 8
Gamification Strategy

Quest
Let's find out how to identify learning objectives, learner characteristics, and motivators.
Let's understand a gamification process for our classrooms.
Let's figure out how to embed principles of games in our classrooms.

8.1 Manpower Planning and Development Process

Manpower planning is one of the important functions for almost every organization. It might be more significant for teams developing specific products and services than other types of teams because the development teams usually have limited time to launch the product and service. Also, each of the team members must be an expert in each field.

8.1.1 Manpower Planning

Gamification requires experts from a variety of fields. Kapp (2012) suggests a manpower planning model for gamification. The model consists of ten groups: project manager, instructional game designer, subject matter expert, artist, music and sound technician, animator, level designer, programmer, information technology representative, and representative of learner population. The following are the roles and responsibilities of each group:

- Project manager
  - Responsible for the management of all phases of a gamification project
  - Assigns responsibilities to each member
  - Facilitates communication
  - Responsible for the quality of the final products

S. Kim et al., *Gamification in Learning and Education*, Advances in Game-Based Learning, DOI 10.1007/978-3-319-47283-6_8

- Instructional game designer
  - Provides expertise in the field of instructional systems design
  - Designs instructional systems and learning materials based on associated learning theories
- Subject matter expert
  - Provides expertise in the field related to the content
  - Provides content for gamification
- Artist
  - Develops game aesthetics
  - Aligns aesthetics to game characteristics
- Music/sound technician
  - Creates background music and sound effects, which provide gamers feedback and messages informing them of what they can/need to do
- Animator
  - Designs the mechanisms that allow game characters and other game elements to move
- Level designer
  - Designs missions and challenges for each game level
- Programmer
  - Writes codes to make games work as designed
- Information technology representative
  - Provides expertise on the technical requirements to run a game
  - Ensures new game-based learning will run on the organization's existing system and other infrastructures
- Representative of learner population
  - Provides input representing the target learner
  - Provides feedback on game effectiveness and learner comfort

Purdue University (2007) suggested a somewhat simplified manpower planning model for an educational game development team.

- Subject matter expert (SME)
  - Provides the instructional content for the game
  - Identifies the learning objectives
  - Supplies assessment metrics

- Instructional designer
  - Designs instructional strategies that achieve the objectives
- Game designer
  - Creates game elements, such as rules and rewards, at the pre-production stages
  - Provides the production team with a detailed roadmap
  - Plays the role of a writer or director in a film
- Programmer
  - Writes the programming codes to make the game function as desired
  - Programming duties vary depending on the detail programming field
- Artist
  - Produces the models, textures, user interfaces, and animations
- Technical director
  - Expertise in the art production pipeline as well as programming
  - Writes custom tools for the artists
  - Serves as technical liaison between the programmers and artists

Manpower planning suggested by Kapp (2012) and Purdue University (2007) assumes that gamification for education can be implemented in the form of software and requires hardware and network systems. So, the gamification exists in a web or mobile app game, not a board game or war game. Due to this assumption, the manpower planning of Kapp (2012) and Purdue University (2007) does not include some roles that are necessary for gamification development projects when interpreting the definition of gamification in a broad sense. If the game is a type of board game, the manpower plan should include a tool developer. Also, if the development project needs a large budget, budget and cost management should be one of the roles in the development project. If the scope of development project includes an improvement phase, performance evaluation can be included in the project as one of the roles. Table 8.1 describes roles and responsibilities for the gamification development project. A project member can be in charge of multiple roles.

8.1.2 Development Process

There are various models and processes that can be used for gamification development projects (Mora, Riera, González, & Arnedo-Moreno, 2017). The ADDIE model, one of the most representative instructional design models, can be considered to develop games for educational settings. Branson et al. (1975) created the

Table 8.1 Manpower planning for gamification development projects

Roles	Responsibilities	Notes
Project manager	Manages project scope, schedule, cost, quality, manpower planning, communication, risk management, and resource provision Communicates with clients	
Subject matter expert	Provides content Reviews final outcome	
Instructional designer	Designs instructional strategies and learning processes Determines if game dynamics and mechanics are in accord with the instructional strategies	
Story designer	Creates stories for gamification	
Game designer	Designs game dynamics and mechanics Determines if implemented games and tools are in accord with the game mechanics	
Programmer	Develops game software Integrates game software with existing systems	Mostly for game software development projects
Graphic designer	Creates 2D and 3D graphics Creates avatars, characters, and background images	
Music/sound technician	Composes background music Produces sound effects	Mostly for game software development projects
Tool developer	Develops tools for gamification in the form of board games or war games Makes printed materials, dice, game boards, and other types of tools	Limited roles in game software development projects
Quality manager	Manages the quality of the work in process and the final product Manages each test phase (alpha, beta, and pilot)	
Information technology representative	Knows existing IT systems and integrates new game software with the existing systems Solves information security issues	Mostly for game software development projects
Representative of target learner population	Participates in all development phases and suggests opinions from the user perspective	More representatives can provide more various opinions

ADDIE model, consisting of analysis, design, development, implementation, and evaluation phases, for the US Army. The model has evolved over the years. Each phase is explained as follows:

- Analysis phase: The analysis phase is a front-end analysis which includes analyzing business needs, performance, performance requirements/gaps, training/instruction needs, learner characteristics, learners' existing knowledge, learning environments, and preference of learning methods.
- Design phase: The design phase involves identifying the learning objectives, evaluation criteria, entry behaviors, and details of the learning process. An instructional designer can design an instruction based on the results of the analysis phase. The design phase provides the development phase with the detailed basis.

- Development phase: An instructional design becomes operationalized at the development phase. The development phase produces learning materials, such as instructional media and performance aids. Also, an instructional designer develops evaluation tools.
- Implementation phase: Instruction is delivered to the learners at the implementation phase. The instruction delivery method can vary depending on the characteristics of learners and learning contexts. It can be a classroom instruction, an e-learning module, or simulation software.
- Evaluation phase: An instructional designer or a design team evaluates the instruction with the goal of identifying opportunities to improve it. Trainers and instructors who delivered the instruction can participate in this phase and share their experience with those who designed or will re-design the instruction to improve the performance of the instruction and achieve its objectives.

Some gamification development projects may develop a game software to meet their clients' needs. The projects can direct more focus on the game software development process. Purdue University (2007) suggested a game development process. This process includes Pre-Production phase, Production phase, and Post-Production phase.

Game designers, subject matter experts, and instructional designers are involved in the Pre-Production phase to establish the game concepts and components and design an instruction using the game. At the Production phase, artists, programmers, and technical directors implement the game. Professional and beta testers and educational specialists assess the fun aspects and effectiveness of the game at the Post-Production phase. After the tests, the game can be deployed for the target audiences.

A gamification development process in this book integrates the ADDIE model (Branson et al., 1975) and Game Development Process of Purdue University (2007). The gamification development process consists of five phases: Gamification Target Analysis, Gamification Element Design, Development, Deployment and Implementation, and Evaluation and Improvement (see Fig. 8.1).

8.2 Gamification Target Analysis

8.2.1 Instructional Objective Identification

Instructions should have specific objectives based on instructional needs and/or performance gaps. Thus, it is necessary to understand what the instructional needs are and/or how performance meets the needs as a first step for a gamification development project.

For identifying instructional needs and/or performance gaps, instructional designers frequently use the records and data regarding the expected or planned level of performance and the actual level of performance (Morschheuser, Werder, Hamari, & Abe, 2017). In other words, they evaluate current performance trends compared to desired performance trends. The gap between the two is where they will direct their attention in their objective identification. In some situations, they measure and evaluate performance themselves to use more accurate data.

Phases	Activities	Involved Members
Gamification Target Analysis	▪ Identify needs, objectives, and scope ▪ Analyze characteristics of learners and learning environments	• Project manager • Instructional designer • Subject matter expert • Representative of learner population
Gamification Element Design	▪ Design motivational strategies ▪ Design story and dynamics ▪ Design mechanics	• Project manager • Instructional designer • Story designer / Game designer
Development	▪ Develop programs ▪ Create graphics and sounds ▪ Develop and test tools	• Project manager / Quality manager • Programmer / Graphic designer • Sound technician / Tool developer • IT representative
Deployment & Implementation	▪ Deploy the game ▪ Implement the game ▪ Monitor the instruction using the game	• Project manager • Information technology representative
Evaluation & Improvement	▪ Evaluate the learning achievement and fun of the instruction ▪ Improve the game and the instruction	• Project manager / Quality manager • Subject matter expert • Representative of learner population

Fig. 8.1 Gamification development process

The instructional objective is a description of expected results and performance of instruction and learning. The instructional objective can be articulated based on the instructional needs and performance gap analyses. The instructional objectives should include the information on the audience, behavior, conditions, and degree. The audience describes who will learn and perform. The behavior specifies what the learners will be able to do. The behaviors in the instructional objective must be observable. The instructional objective also contains the conditions under which the learners will perform a specific task. Lastly, the degree of the behavioral mastery should be included in the instructional objective to define the expected performance level.

8.2.2 *Definition of Gamification Scope*

The target and scope of gamification should be defined at this step. The project members involved in this step should consider the following:

- What topics or subjects interest students the least?
- What topics or subjects are students struggling to maintain in their long-term memory?
- What can be learned more effectively by interactions with other learners?

Depending on the answers to the above questions, the scope of the gamification project can vary. Some projects may only need to focus on one item, but others may require applying the gamification to all activities in the instruction which will expand the gamification scope substantially.

8.2.3 Analysis of Learner Characteristics

Instructional designers analyze the characteristics of the learner population. They investigate the game experience and game player types. While investigating the game experience of the learners, the instructional designers can see the preferred fun perspectives of games. In the previous chapters, the studies by Apter (1991), Bartle (2003), Caillois (2001), Costello and Edmonds (2007), Csikszentmihalyi (1975), Hunicke, LeBlanc, and Zubek. (2004), Kubovy (1999), Poels, De Kort, and Ijsselsteijn (2007), Sweetser and Wyeth (2005), and Yee (2002) have described the details of and the ways to identify the preferred fun perspectives of games. Instructional designers can use those studies or the PLEX model by Korhonen, Montola, and Arrasvunori (2009). The PLEX model (Korhonen et al., 2009) consists of 20 fun perspectives of games: Captivation, Challenge, Completion, Competition, Control, Discovery, Eroticism, Exploration, Expression, Fantasy, Fellowship, Nurture, Sadism, Sensation, Simulation, Submission, Subversion, Suffering, Sympathy, and Thrill.

For identifying game player types, eight types categorized by Bartle (2005) can be used. The eight player types include Griefer, Opportunist, Networker, Scientist, Politician, Planner, Friend, and Hacker Bartle (2005). The information gained from the learner characteristic analysis can be used for designing gamification elements and story.

8.3 Gamification Element Design

8.3.1 Motivational Strategy

The motivational strategy plays an important role in learner engagement with the instruction. Instructional designers can consider the intrinsic and extrinsic motivation (Deci & Ryan, 2000; Taylor et al., 2014), Self-Determination theory (Deci & Ryan, 2008), Achievement Goal Theory (Dweck & Leggett, 1988; Elliott & Dweck, 1988), Social Learning Theory (Bandura, 1977), Situated Learning Theory (Lave, 1988), and feedback to design the motivational strategies.

For instance, if the learners have strong esteem and belonging needs, the instructional designers should embed the device to meet the esteem and belonging needs in the motivational strategy.

8.3.2 Story and Dynamics Design

Before starting to design story and dynamics for the gamification, it can be useful to review the 12 stage Hero's Journey model described by Vogler and Montez (2007) to draw the backbone of the story and dynamics. The information on the preferred fun perspectives of games and the game player types can be used for determining the structure of the story.

It is not necessary for the game and story designer to cover all of the game player types and the preferred fun perspectives of games. It is important, however, to prioritize the game player types and preferred fun perspectives of games found in the learner population.

8.3.3 Mechanics Design

The goal of mechanics design is to create a more detailed story and dynamics and to provide project members involved in the development phase with the story and dynamics in a usable format. Table 8.2 describes the elements for gamification mechanics. The game designer can use some or all of the listed elements for the game mechanics (Chang & Wei, 2016).

For the projects developing tools rather than game software, the game designer can use the principles for the game design suggested by Tinsman (2008).

- Playing Time: The players must have an appropriate period of time for the play. If they don't have enough time to play the game, they can't experience the game enough. On the contrary, if they have too much time to play the game, the learning effect will be reduced.
- Critical Decision Making Factors: It is important to clarify what critical decision making is in the game design. For example, trading real estate is critical decision making in the Monopoly game.

Table 8.2 Elements for gamification mechanics

Categories	Elements
Rewards	Points, levels, progression, badge, authority, virtual items, physical goods, severance, gifting, free items, virtual money
Reward schedules	Fixed interval reward schedules, fixed ratio reward schedules, variable interval reward schedules, variable ratio reward schedules
Avoidance	Disincentives, leaky bucket
Leader board	Macro leaderboard, micro leaderboard, indirect competition, direct competition
Status	Avatar, social graph
Quests	Content unlocking, countdown, lottery, communal discovery, scaffolding

- Documentation of Rules: The rules of the game should be easy to understand without additional explanation.
- Stakes, Risks, and Rewards: The game players can receive rewards and a feeling of satisfaction for their efforts and investment in learning and playing the game.
- Luck Versus Strategy: Embedding luck to the game can relieve the mental pressure of the player, but if luck influences the game too much, the player will lose the fun that can be gained by making strategic decisions.
- Feedback: The information on the progress and game results of each player should be shared within the game arena to keep dramatic tension.
- Catch-up Features: There should be chances to catch up by luck, magic, or making strategic decisions. If there is no chance to catch up, the player may feel bored.
- Meeting General Anticipation and Expectation: It is too risky making the structure and elements of the game strange.

A virtual economy can be constructed within the game that is based on principles of economy systems as the size of the game grows. The virtual economy often includes a barter system, gifting, or even virtual money. The game designer can consider the virtual money for the following situations (Radoff, 2011).

- Reward: Virtual money can be awarded to the game player who successfully completes specific missions and quests. Figure 8.2 illustrates a mission in

Fig. 8.2 Building a Parisian building as a mission in SimCity BuildIt (Reproduced from SimCity BuildIt, Copyright 2013 by Electronic Arts Inc)

SimCity BuildIt (Electronic Arts Inc., 2013), which is to build a Parisian building. Players who complete this mission receive rewards, such as increasing population, virtual currency, and level point.

- Salary: The game player can get paid for logging-in the game or playing the game for a specific period of time.
- Reselling: When the game player sells virtual goods through a store in the game, the player can receive virtual money. In SimCity BuildIt (Electronic Arts Inc., 2013) game, each player can resell virtual goods through Global Trade HQ and Trade Depot (see Figs. 8.3 and 8.4).

SimCity BuildIt (Electronic Arts Inc., 2013) provides game players with Global Trade HQ and Trade Depot to promote a virtual economy system, and the players can buy virtual goods they want or sell surplus goods via this system. Some players make profits by selling goods at a higher price than the purchase price. This type of economy system is designed and implemented in a way similar to the real-world system.

- Purchase: The game player can purchase virtual money for the game with real money. In SimCity BuildIt, the player can buy SimCash with real money (see Fig. 8.5).

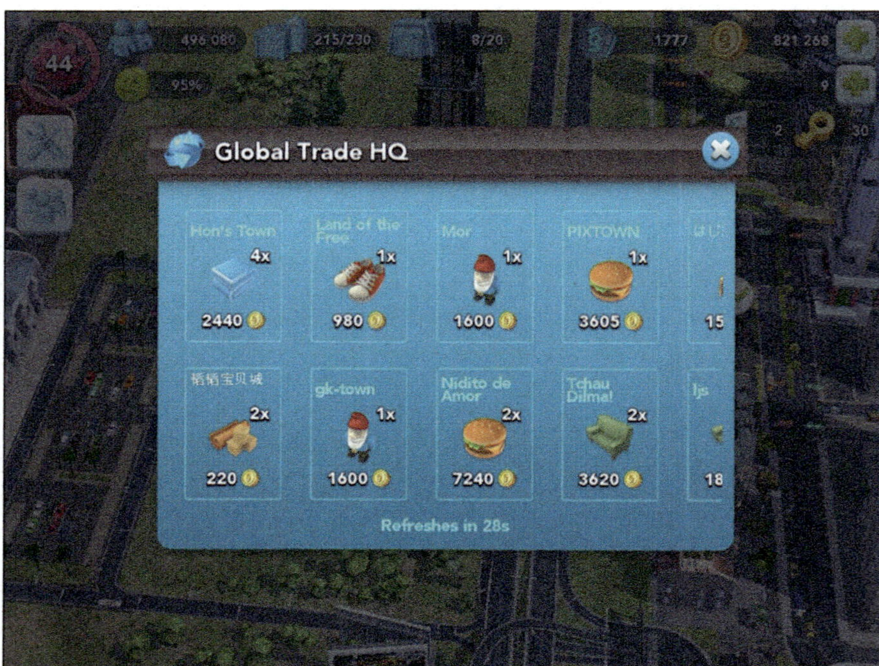

Fig. 8.3 Global Trade HQ in SimCity BuildIt (Reproduced from SimCity BuildIt, Copyright 2013 by Electronic Arts Inc.)

Fig. 8.4 Trade Depot in SimCity BuildIt (Reproduced from SimCity BuildIt, Copyright 2013 by Electronic Arts Inc)

The virtual economy system can reflect similar problems that can occur in real-world economy systems. Radoff (2011) pointed out that kind of problems (see Table 8.3).

As a virtual economy system, virtual money will be explained later in this chapter.

TIP. An attempt by Coca Cola to apply the principles of market forces
In 1999, Coca Cola had an interesting idea which is to sell its soda at a higher price on hot days by embedding a temperature sensor to vending machine. It seemed quite reasonable in terms of an economic law, the law of demand and supply.

Unlike the anticipation of Coca Cola, customers blamed the new attempt of Coca Cola since they perceived the change as a sort of the exploitation of customers.

This is a case that price fairness perception worked. When customers determine the price propriety of a good, they consider their past experience and current conditions.

8.4 Development

This phase is to develop working games based on the design. The first step of this phase is to decide the game type: game software or a physical game. The development process can vary depending on the game type (see Fig. 8.6).

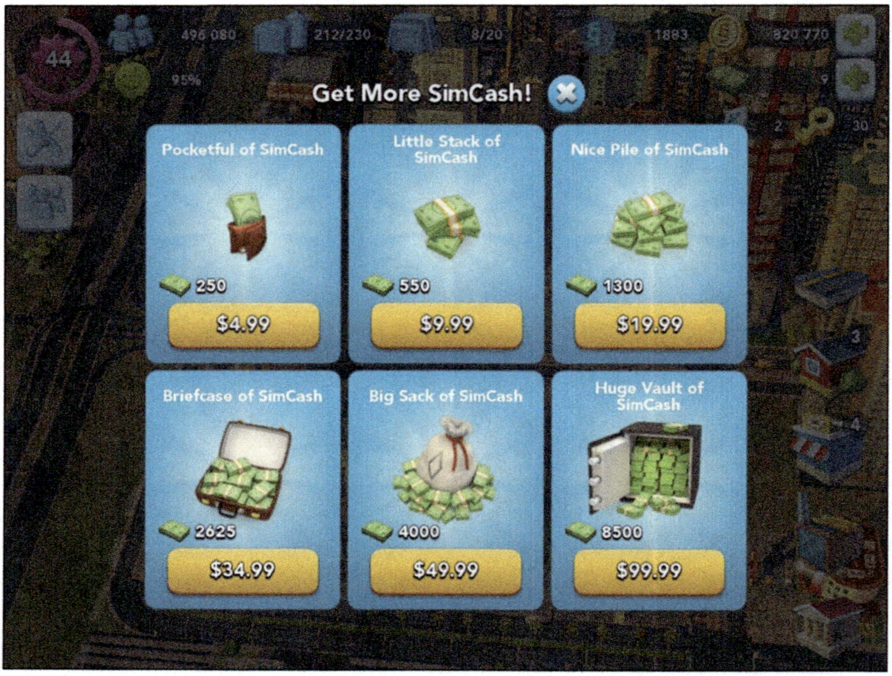

Fig. 8.5 SimCash purchase in SimCity BuildIt (Reproduced from SimCity BuildIt, Copyright 2013 by Electronic Arts Inc)

Table 8.3 Problems in virtual economy systems

Problems	Description	Solutions
Hyperinflation	Game players don't perceive the value of virtual goods and lose interest in playing the game	Reduce the virtual money supply or make players spend more money
Depression	Game players can't make money enough to purchase virtual goods. Continuous depression can make players discouraged	Increase the virtual money supply or diversify economy systems by adding new virtual goods
Inequality	Due to the structural defect of the game, economic inequality exists. If there is no chance to overcome this inequality, players will feel angry	Make various paths to take economic dominance or add alternative options to catch up with other players
Black market	Black market is an unplanned place to trade goods. It is outside the control of the game manager	Provide more various markets that can meet players' needs

If the gamification project develops game software, it is necessary to integrate the game software with the existing systems of the client in many cases. For example, the newly developed game for educating accountants in a particular state may need to be integrated into an existing learning management system of that state. In a case such as this, the information technology representative

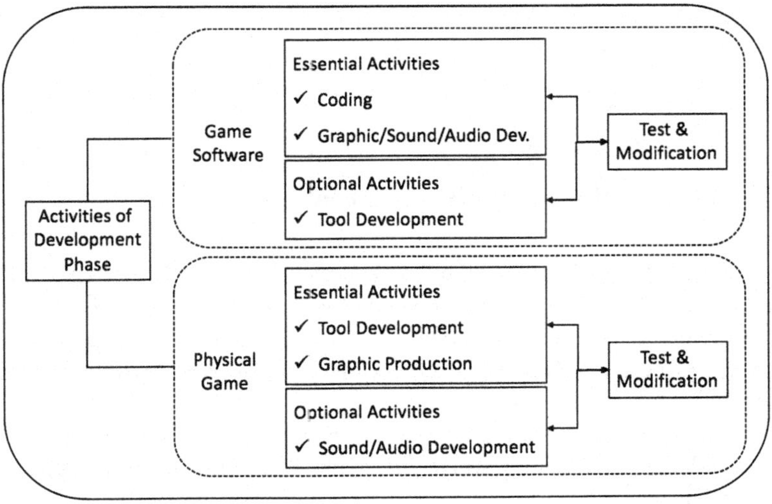

Fig. 8.6 A development process for a gamification project

at the client organization should support the development process by providing following:

- Classify accessible data
- Authorize data access
- Manage security and risks
- Provide APIs for migration and integration
- Solve problems caused by system failure

After developing a game, it is necessary to have them alpha and beta tested in order to find problems and improve the game (Fraser, 2017). In gamification development projects for education, project members can be testers for the alpha test and representatives of the learner population can be beta testers.

Tinsman (2008) suggested a test process for physical games like board games.

- Prototype development: Prepare a prototype that can support a game or a game level.
- Unit balancing: Game designers try to play the game themselves and adjust measures of characters, items, and cards (ability, money, possibility).
- Usability test: Gamers play the game and game designers observe gamers and their behaviors to find opportunities to improve the game. This is similar to beta tests.

Tinsman (2008) proposed self-diagnostic questions to be considered when checking the quality of the developed game. The questions are:

- Who is this game for?
- Does this game have the appropriate level of difficulty for the target game players?
- Are the game rules clear?
- Do the game players need to prepare anything before beginning the game?
- Can people play the game with your prototype?

- What factors make people to choose the game?
- Are there similar games?
- Is the game fun?

8.5 Deployment and Implementation

The developed game should be deployed to classrooms or other types of target educational settings. The information technology representative of the client organization should be involved in this phase to carry out the final check and make sure that there will be no problems in running the game software within the existing systems.

After the deployment, the instruction that includes the use of the game may be implemented. Instructors and learners will participate in the implementation phase. The project manager observes the instruction via video recording to review for improvement opportunities. Using a video recording can reduce the pressure that the learners may feel by having an observer present. Sometimes, the project manager participates in the instruction as a learner or observer.

8.6 Evaluation and Improvement

8.6.1 Learning Achievement and Fun

The evaluation phase is to measure, analyze, and interpret learners' behaviors and performance. Though many people think that the development project is complete after implementing the new game, the evaluation and improvement phase is important since there are chances to improve the quality of the game and the instruction that is using it (Heilbrunn, Herzig, & Schill, 2017). Also, the results from the evaluation phase can provide the project team or the client with reasonable evidence of the success of the project.

In game software development projects, the following can be measured, analyzed, and interpreted as part of the evaluation process (Duggan & Shoup, 2013).

- Number of gamers playing the game
- Number of gamers playing the game at specific date and time
- Number of gamers completed given quests
- Distribution of gained points by gamers
- Ratio of gained points by time periods
- Number and distribution of gained rewards by gamers
- Frequency of access to the game
- Rate of increase in playing time
- Number of visits

These evaluation criteria suggested by Duggan and Shoup (2013) can be a part of the analysis feature that gamification platforms provide. Instructors and facilitators can see when, how frequently, and how long learners participate in the instruction. Also, they can find out how many level goals or missions each learner completed. With the answers to the above criteria, however, it is still hard to assess learning achievements. Educators can use survey, interview, test, portfolios, demonstration, or observation for evaluating learning performance.

Measuring the fun that learners felt is simpler than measuring learning performance. Surveys using a Likert-type scale are frequently used for measuring fun. Sometimes, teachers and observers measure fun by observing learners' behaviors.

8.6.2 Improvement

The result of the instruction using gamification can be one of the four results (see Fig. 8.7).

The goal of the gamification development project is to make the instruction "fun and worth learning." If the instruction was neither fun nor worth learning (relevant to the learner), the learners will be less motivated and lose interest in the next lesson (Faghihi et al., 2017). The gamification development project team must review all the phases of the development project and decide if each activity and decisions made were appropriate. If needed, the project should be revised.

If the instruction was worth learning, but not fun, the learners cannot recognize any differences between the instruction using the gamification and traditional instruction. In this case, the project team should check the game dynamics and mechanics of the

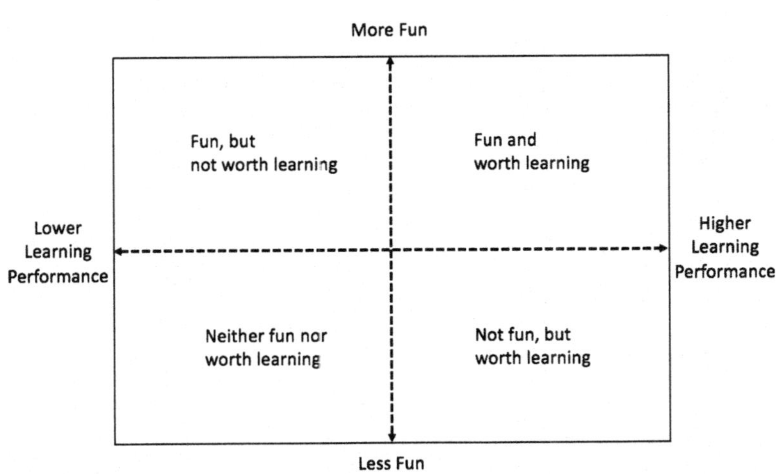

Fig. 8.7 Four results of the instruction using gamification

instruction. If the instruction was fun, but not worth learning, the instructional design embedding the game dynamics and mechanics must be reviewed. In many cases, poor integration of the instructional design and the game dynamics and mechanics can create that type of problem.

References

Apter, M. J. (1991). A structural phenomenology of play. In J. H. Kerr & M. J. Apter (Eds.), *Adult play: A reversal theory approach* (pp. 13–42). Amsterdam, the Netherlands: Swets & Zeitlinger.

Bandura, A. (1977). *Social learning theory*. Englewood Cliffs, NJ: Prentice Hall.

Bartle, R. A. (2003). *Designing virtual worlds*. Indianapolis, IN: New Riders Publishing.

Bartle, R. A. (2005). Virtual worlds: Why people play. In T. Alexander (Ed.), *Massively multiplayer game development 2* (pp. 3–18). Hingham, MA: Charles River Media.

Branson, R. K., Rayner, G. T., Cox, J. L., Furman, J. P., King, F. J., & Hannum, W. H. (1975, August 1). *Interservice procedures for instructional systems development. executive summary and model*. Retrieved from http://www.dtic.mil/

Caillois, R (2001). *Man, play and games*. (M. Barash, Trans.). New York, NY: The Free Press of Glencoe, Inc. (Original work published 1961).

Chang, J. W., & Wei, H. Y. (2016). Exploring engaging gamification mechanics in massive online open courses. *Educational Technology & Society, 19*(2), 177–203.

Costello, B., & Edmonds, E. (2007, August). A study in play, pleasure and interaction design. In *Proceedings of the 2007 Conference on Designing Pleasurable Products and Interfaces* (pp. 76–91). New York, NY: ACM. doi:10.1145/1314161.1314168

Csikszentmihalyi, M. (1975). *Beyond boredom and anxiety*. San Francisco, CA: Josey-Bass.

Deci, E. L., & Ryan, R. M. (2000). The "what" and "why" of goal pursuits: Human needs and the self-determination of behavior. *Psychological Inquiry, 11*, 227–268. doi:10.1207/S15327965PLI1104_01

Deci, E. L., & Ryan, R. M. (2008). Self-determination theory: A macrotheory of human motivation, development, and health. *Canadian Psychology/Psychologie Canadienne, 49*(3), 182.

Duggan, K., & Shoup, K. (2013). *Business gamification for dummies*. Hoboken, NJ: John Wiley & Sons.

Dweck, C. S., & Leggett, E. L. (1988). A social-cognitive approach to motivation and personality. *Psychological Review, 95*(2), 256–273. doi:10.1037/0033-295X.95.2.256

Electronic Arts Inc. (2013). *SimCity BuildIt*. Available from https://www.ea.com/games/simcity/simcity-buildit

Elliott, E. S., & Dweck, C. S. (1988). Goals: An approach to motivation and achievement. *Journal of Personality and Social Psychology, 54*(1), 5–12.

Faghihi, U., Aguilar, D., Chatman, D., Gautier, N., Gholson, J., Gholson, J., … Maldonado-Bouchard, S. (2017). How to apply gamification techniques to design a gaming environment for algebra concepts. In G. Vincenti, A. Bucciero, M. Helfert, & M. Glowatz (Eds.), *E-learning, e-education, and online training: Lecture notes of the Institute for Computer Sciences, social informatics and telecommunications engineering* (Vol. 180, pp. 62–70). Cham, Switzerland: Springer International Publishing.

Fraser, G. (2017, May). *Gamification of software testing*. Paper presented at the 12th International Workshop on Automation of Software Testing (pp. 2–7). doi: 10.1109/AST.2017.20.

Heilbrunn, B., Herzig, P., & Schill, A. (2017). Gamification analytics—Methods and tools for monitoring and adapting gamification designs. In S. Stieglitz, C. Lattemann, S. Robra-Bissantz, R. Zarnekow, & T. Brockmann (Eds.), *Gamification: Using game elements in serious contexts* (pp. 31–47). Cham, Switzerland: Springer International Publishing. doi:10.1007/978-3-319-45557-0

Hunicke, R., LeBlanc, M., & Zubek, R. (2004, July). MDA: A formal approach to game design and game research. In *Proceedings of the AAAI Workshop on Challenges in Game AI* (Vol. 4, No. 1). Retrieved from http://www.cs.northwestern.edu/~hunicke/MDA.pdf

Kapp, K. (2012). *The gamification of learning and instruction: Game-based methods and strategies for training and education*. San Francisco, CA: Pfeiffer.

Korhonen, H., Montola, M., & Arrasvunori, J. (2009). Understanding playful user experience through digital games. In A. Guenand (Ed.), *Proceedings of the 4th International Conference on Designing Pleasurable Products and Interfaces, DPPI 2009* (pp. 274–285). Compiègne, France: ACM Press.

Kubovy, M. (1999). On pleasures of the mind. In D. Kahneman, E. Diener, & N. Schwarz (Eds.), *Well-being: The foundations of hedonic psychology* (pp. 134–154). New York, NY: Russell Sage Foundation.

Lave, J. (1988). *Cognition in practice: Mind, mathematics, and culture in everyday life*. Cambridge, UK: Cambridge University Press.

Mora, A., Riera, D., González, C., & Arnedo-Moreno, J. (2017). Gamification: A systematic review of design frameworks. *Journal of Computing in Higher Education*. doi:10.1007/s12528-017-9150-4

Morschheuser, B., Werder, K., Hamari, J., & Abe, J. (2017, January). *How to gamify? Development of a method for gamification*. Paper presented at the 50th Annual Hawaii International Conference on System Sciences (HICSS). http://hdl.handle.net/10125/41308

Poels, K., De Kort, Y., & Ijsselsteijn, W. (2007, November). "It is always a lot of fun!" exploring dimensions of digital game experience using focus group methodology. In *Proceedings of the 2007 Conference on Future Play* (pp. 83–89). New York, NY: ACM.

Purdue University. (2007). *Game development process*. Retrieved from https://e-games.tech.purdue.edu

Radoff, J. (2011). *Game on: Energize your business with social media games*. Indianapolis, IN: Wiley Publishing.

Sweetser, P., & Wyeth, P. (2005). GameFlow: A model for evaluating player enjoyment in games. *ACM Computers in Entertainment (CIE)*, *3*(3), 1–24.

Taylor, G., Jungert, T., Mageau, G. A., Schattke, K., Dedic, H., Rosenfield, S., & Koestner, R. (2014). A self-determination theory approach to predicting school achievement over time: The unique role of intrinsic motivation. *Contemporary Educational Psychology*, *39*(4), 342–358.

Tinsman, B. (2008). *The game inventor's guidebook: How to invent and sell board games, card games, role-playing games, & everything in between*. Garden City, NY: Morgan James Publishing.

Vogler, C., & Montez, M. (2007). *The writer's journey: Mythic structure for writers* (3rd ed.). Studio City, CA: Michael Wiese Productions.

Yee, N. (2002). *Facets: 5 motivation factors for why people play MMORPG's*. Retrieved from http://www.nickyee.com

Chapter 9
Legal and Ethical Issues

Quest
Let's explore legal issues in gamification.
Let's figure out ethical issues in dynamics and mechanics.
Let's understand side effects of gamification.

9.1 Legal Issues

Since each country and state have different laws, it is hard to explain universal rules that can be applied for every setting and situation. However, this section will discuss some legal issues that can occur in many places.

9.1.1 Privacy

The concept of privacy is somewhat vague and its definition varies depending on disciplines. However, regardless of disciplines, it is a commonly acceptable idea that privacy cannot exist without the cooperation of people and society.

Problems related to privacy occur when unauthorized individuals or unaccredited organizations access or try to access the personal information of an individual or a group. In the course of designing or running gamified learning and education, educators may need to use students' personal information. Educators should not assume that they have the right to use the information even though they may have access to it. When personal information is used for different purposes than originally intended, educators must acquire permission. To avoid privacy issues, it is necessary to ask following questions:

S. Kim et al., *Gamification in Learning and Education*, Advances in Game-Based Learning, DOI 10.1007/978-3-319-47283-6_9

- Are you authorized to access the personal information?
- Do you have an official document proving permission to access the personal information?
- Do you have a safe means to protect the personal information?
- Are there any individuals who can access the personal information without permission?
- Does the personal information include private information like social security numbers?
- Do you have a contingency plan for data spillage?

Unless the gamification in learning and education is for anonymous learners, it collects and uses identifiable information, such as user IDs. Encrypting data is highly recommended when it is unavoidable to collect and use the identifiable information.

If gamification uses information technologies, there is higher possibility of invading privacy rights. Gamification based on information technologies sometimes includes user tracking techniques such as the following:

- Cookies
- IP addresses
- Device IDs
- GPS coordinate data
- Log data on user behaviors (e.g., visited pages and duration)
- Log data on user's technological environment (e.g., web browser and operating system)
- Analytics

While analytics from the above list is for analyzing data, the others are for collecting data that can be used as user tracking. Using cookies is not a new technology. Cookies are created by the activity on web browsers and stored in a user's computer. The gamification system accesses and uses the stored cookies when the user accesses it. Some gamification systems use IP addresses to see user's geographical location or network environments. If the gamification uses mobile devices, the system for gamification can collect GPS coordinate data showing the student's moving paths.

Analytics tools provide educators with meaningful information in terms of education. The information includes:

- When and how frequently each student accesses the gamification system or gamified learning materials
- Access history with visited pages and stay time on each page
- What technological environments each student has

Educators have to check what kinds of technologies will be used for the gamification and inform students some technologies will be used for the gamified learning and education. Also, when educators use leaderboards for the gamification, they need to consider how the leaderboards will be shared and what information will be included in them. Some students may not want to show their real names on the leaderboard.

9.1.2 Copyright

Copyright is a legal protection device to ensure creators' rights regarding the use of their work. Copyright, as a protection means, can promote creative works in various fields. However, copyright issues sometimes delay the development process for gamification. Educators must beware that it is illegal to use existing avatars, virtual items, or badges in most cases. Those are protected by copyright. Thus, educators need to create their own avatars, virtual items, and badges. Or they have to request and acquire the permission to use existing works. Although many copyright holders allow educators to use their creative works for educational purposes, it should not be assumed that educators can use the creative works without permission.

When educators want to use some old works, they need to check if the copyright for the works has lapsed. According to the Berne Convention for the Protection of Literary and Artistic Works, which is an international treaty signed in 1886, most creative works are protected for 50 years after the creator's death (for the duration of the creator's life plus 50 years.) However, some countries protect the copyright for different durations. Many countries protect the copyright for 70 years after the creator's death.

Unlike applied art works including avatars, virtual items, and badges, the game mechanics and rules are usually not protected by copyright. It is because accepting exclusive rights for the game mechanics and rules can hinder other creative efforts for developing games and gamification.

It is recommended that educators contact the copyright holder to discuss permission and possible monetary compensation before starting to develop the gamification.

Online Resources for Further Studies on Copyright Laws:

- *World Intellectual Property Organization at www.wipo.int*
- *WTO* TRIPS** Agreement at www.wto.org/english/tratop_e/trips_e/t_agm0_e.htm*
- *US Copyright Office at www.copyright.gov*
- *EU Intellectual Property Office at euipo.europa.eu*
- *UK Intellectual Property Office at ipo.gov.uk*

**WTO: World Trade Organization.*
***TRIPS: Trade-Related Aspects of Intellectual Property Rights.*

9.1.3 Ownership

Educators may encounter ownership issues while running the gamification, although this type of issue is not frequent. Game players invest their time and resources in games or gamified systems for making progress and achieving goals. Their progresses and achievements are usually managed in the form of data. However, the data can be affected by unexpected situations such as the following:

- Network failures in sending data on the player's action to the gamification system
- Programming error that causes data distortion
- Loss of data on specific player's or entire players' progresses and achievements

When the gamification uses information technologies, educators should check the reliability of the technologies by conducting pilot tests with authentic scenarios. It is not easy to find and fix the cause of the technological problems during running the gamification.

Even when the gamification does not use gamification systems based on information technologies, loss of data can occur during or after the gamification. Though it is not frequent, losing data on the player's progress and achievement makes the player discouraged and suspicious of the gamification's reliability. The player who experiences loss of data has a tendency to stop participating in the gamification in the future.

Ownership is not an issue when the gamification works without any problems. When loss of data occurs, however, the ownership becomes an issue. In many cases, users sign an agreement on the terms and conditions of the game and gamification services. The agreement usually includes phrases clarifying the ownership of the data or virtual items belonging to those who operate the game or gamification. Based on the agreement, game companies may argue that users do not have ownership of the data and virtual items. In opposition, users may claim that the ownership should belong to the users since the data and virtual items are the products of their efforts and investments.

Ownership issues become more serious when the data and virtual items are valuable in the real world. Some games and gamification platforms include items that have exchange values in the real world since the inclusion of them can encourage the players more. This means that losing player progress and achievement data is no longer just a problem within the gamification. The player, as a victim, may ask those who operate the gamification for appropriate compensation for their loss. Some countries accept players' ownership of virtual items and their value as property.

9.2 Ethical Issues

While legal issues are related to rules that can have penalties when violated, ethical issues are not directly associated with penalties (Thorpe & Roper, 2017). However, educators should know the ethical issues, including justification, deception, and consent, that can occur while developing and running the gamification.

9.2.1 Justification

Who defines the rules of the gamification in learning and education? In most cases, educators decide the rules except for the cases when students participate in the gamification design. However, some rules can be against some of the students due to their social, cultural, and educational environments and their physical conditions.

Educators need to check the game rules in terms of justification when they design the gamification. They have to review the data on their target audiences, namely their students. If it is hard to remove the rule that can be against some of the students, educators should consider including alternatives that can be optionally selected by each student.

Another type of justification issue is associated with the possibility of inducing students to take a specific action or have a particular preference that is not related to the purpose of the gamification. For example, when the gamified education includes a means to form a student's preference on a specific tablet computer, some people, including students, may raise the justification issue.

9.2.2 Deception

Deception is an action to achieve a goal by providing an individual or organization with incorrect information that is necessary to make a decision. In gamification in learning and education, deception may occur if students are misled about the purpose of the technologies used for and mechanics used in the gamification.

Although the American Psychological Association permits deception for psychological experiments, educators should provide students with sufficient and correct information and intentionally avoid deceiving students in gamification.

Many fields, including medicine and psychology, allow the deception of patients or experiment participants with some limitations because there can be benefits. In education, likewise, deception can be considered to confer a benefit to students. If deception is necessary for achieving educational goals of the gamification, educators may consider deception after trying to find the alternatives that can be used for achieving the same goals. Deception should be the last option educators choose. When educators use deception for their gamification, it is recommended to have an internal review committee that reviews the gamification plan and assures the students' rights and risks.

9.2.3 Consent

Consent is a familiar process to educators since they have used it for special activities such as research, field trips, or information use. It is best to follow the consent process before running the gamification especially when students have not experienced the gamification before. Educators should provide students and their parents, if the students are at K-12 schools, with the details on the gamification and what the students will do within the gamified education.

Some gamified education may include participants other than students. If it is necessary to include those who are neither educators nor students in gamification, the consent process is significant. Before acquiring the consent, educators should inform all participants of possible situations and risks that may arise during the gamification.

9.2.4 *Limitation of Acceptable Fun*

As discussed in the previous chapters of the book, there are various fun types in games and gamification. However, some fun types are inappropriate for learning and education although they can be more fun than the others. For example, eroticism, sadism, and subversion are the fun types that educators should avoid in their gamification. When the gamification includes young students, the educator needs to be more careful to decide the fun types for the gamification.

9.3 Side Effects

Incomplete gamification can cause side effects. Some side effects are difficult to interpret before running the gamification. Thus, educators should pilot test and review any possible side effects. They should also consider including a means to reduce the side effects when they are unavoidable.

9.3.1 *Pointsification*

Many gamifications include points as one of the game mechanics. Some people think that the users of an information system or a program will be satisfied with game points as an additional feature to the legacy system or program. The new feature, however, reduces the user's fun.

Robertson (2010) defines pointsification as "taking the thing that is least essential to games and representing it as the core of the experience." Below is Robertson's comment on pointsification.

> Points and badges have no closer a relationship to games than they do to websites and fitness apps and loyalty cards. They're great tools for communicating progress and acknowledging effort, but neither points nor badges in any way constitute a game. Games just use them – as primary school teachers, military hierarchies and coffee shops have for centuries – to help people visualise things they might otherwise lose track of. They are the least important bit of a game, the bit that has the least to do with all of the rich cognitive, emotional and social drivers which gamifiers are intending to connect with.

Some educators may consider awarding game points to the students who come to the class on time for their gamified classes. However, are the students interested in this kind of game points? The game point as extrinsic motivation is not a bad idea, but the gamification can be more effective when it includes both intrinsic and extrinsic motivation (Colby, 2017).

Google News users could earn badges by reading news articles on Google News. However, there were so many badges and it was not hard to earn the badges. As a result, the users perceived that the badge is valueless. They could not feel a sense of accomplishment, fellowship, and fun. Google seems to have overlooked the fact that people consider the meaning and story of virtual items as being more important than the virtual items themselves.

9.3.2 Dangerous Gamification

Players' behaviors in the gamification are sometimes unpredictable. Players tend to find more efficient ways to achieve their goals. Some of the ways found by players are not intended to be included in the gamification. Players finding new ways may be an embarrassment to the gamification designer or educator. However, more importantly, some of the ways found by the players increase the risk of the failure of the gamification and put the players at risk.

The risk becomes more serious when the gamification is integrated with the player's life beyond the gamification. Lazzaro (2012) explained the gamification for the Bay Bridge traffic as an example of the risk. To solve the traffic problem during the rush hour, the game designer suggested having a different toll rate, charging $6 before 7 PM and $4 from 7 PM. After implementing the gamification, the drivers found a way to save their money. Some drivers pulled their vehicles over off the highway to wait until 7 PM and save $2. The unpredicted behavior increased the risk of accidents.

In education, it is possible to observe similar phenomena. Educators may consider using the following techniques to avoid possible risks:

- Ask students about how to achieve their goals
- Draw a flow chart describing all possible behaviors within the gamification
- Remove or minimize the possible behaviors outside the classroom
- Conduct pilot tests

9.3.3 Threat to Core Values

The feedback and rewards in the gamification can weaken students' intrinsic motivation (Burke & Hiltbrand, 2011; Groh, 2012). Students who think virtual currency, points, and badges as valueless may perceive that their efforts and achievements are underestimated due to the rewards by the gamification. Activities in the gamification can be hampered by some of them because they think their teacher infantilizes them.

To prevent this type of problem, educators should explain that the feedback and reward are complementary to the gamified learning and its evaluation system. Also, they should correctly reflect students' efforts and achievements on their feedback and rewards. Compared to the real efforts and achievements, excessive rewards can make students lose interest in the gamification. On the other hand, if it is too hard to acquire the rewards, students will give up the learning or have a complaint about the rules of the gamification.

References

Burke, M., & Hiltbrand, T. (2011). How gamification will change business intelligence. *Business Intelligence Journal, 16*(2), 8–16.

Colby, R. S. (2017). Game-based pedagogy in the writing classroom. *Computers and Composition, 43*, 55–72.

Groh, F. (2012). Gamification: State of the art definition and utilization. In *Proceedings of the 4th seminar on Research Trends in Media Informatics* (pp. 39–46). Ulm, Germany: Institute of Media Informatics Ulm University.

Lazzaro, N. (2012, March 23). *Gamification can kill.* Nicole Lazzaro's Blog. Retrieved from http://www.nicolelazzaro.com/gamification/

Robertson, M. (2010, October 6). *Can't play, won't play.* Hide & Seek. Retrieved from http://hideandseek.net/2010/10/06/cant-play-wont-play/

Thorpe, A. S., & Roper, S. (2017). The ethics of gamification in a marketing context. *Journal of Business Ethics*. doi:10.1007/s10551-017-3501-y

Chapter 10
Gamification Cases in Education

Quest

Let's explore gamification cases in education field.
Let's understand how educators use gamification for their classes.
Let's figure out tools or systems to support gamification in education.

10.1 Just Press Play

In 2012, the School of Interactive Games and Media at Rochester Institute of Technology developed Just Press Play (2012) to help students engage in learning and learning environments. Students who participate in Just Press Play can improve their academic performance, make their lives easier, and improve their happiness (Werbach & Hunter, 2012).

With Just Press Play (2012), students are able to have rapport with and receive advice from their professors, get familiar with campus, develop collaboration skills, and form study groups (Werbach & Hunter, 2012). For these, students collect cards after conducting specific activities:

- Visiting their professor's room and trying to find cards during the meeting
- Collaborating with team members to pass a programming test
- Writing on a blog
- Developing a 3D game with other classmates

There are two axes representing students' experience points in Just Press Play (2012). On the horizontal axis is the "I-We" axis and on the vertical axis is the "Explore-Master" axis. From the two axes, students' experience points can be classified into four areas: "I-Explore," "I-Master," "We-Explore," and "We-Master" (see Fig. 10.1).

Writing on a blog is an activity that can belong to the "I-Explore" area. Developing a 3D game with other classmates can be considered as an activity in the "We-Master"

S. Kim et al., *Gamification in Learning and Education*, Advances in Game-Based Learning, DOI 10.1007/978-3-319-47283-6_10

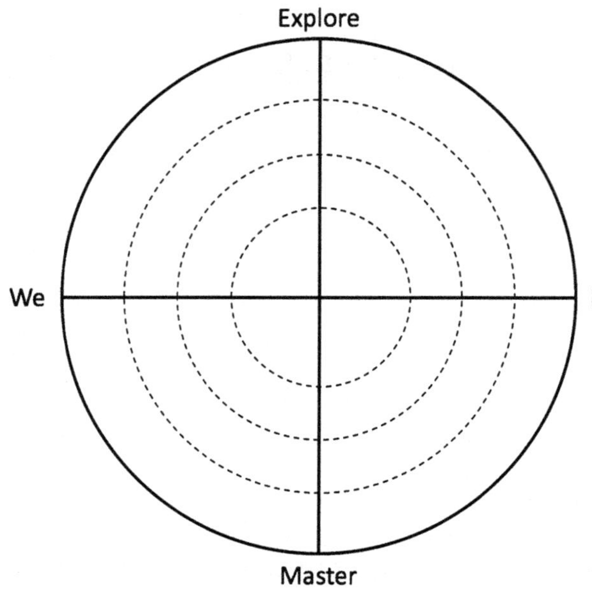

Fig. 10.1 Experience point in Just Press Play

area. This type of mechanism helps to promote and develop students' individual abilities and collaboration skills. Students are encouraged to not just gain knowledge in one specific domain or master a particular skill, but also explore new knowledge and gain several new skills.

Just Press Play (2012) is based on activities in the real world, and some of its features use information technology. For example, Just Press Play uses Radio Frequency Identification (RFID) to collect the information on the student's location and moving paths. The RFID is embedded in a key chain that the student carries. Also, the sensors installed on the campus detect the RFID. With these technologies, it is possible to trace the student's location and whom the student is with. The information collected by the RFID is integrated with the systems at the school to make it more meaningful.

Just Press Play (2012) is considered one of the successful gamification cases in the education field.

10.2 Who is Herring Hale?

In 2006, the University of Brighton developed the "Who is Herring Hale?", an alternate reality game, designed to help freshmen orient themselves to college life and improve engagement (Piatt, 2009). Although any student can participate in the game, the students who achieved at least 70% on a quiz receive an invitation letter to the game.

The first trial of the game was made during the 2006/2007 academic year. The game consisted of 10 quests. The students received a quest each week during a semes-

Table 10.1 Tasks and department in "Who is Herring Hale?"

Week	Task	Department
0	New student quiz	General
1	Locate a desk load book and find a specific name	Library
2	Find and apply for a specific job	Careers
3	Decode a clue hidden in the meals vouchers	Catering
4	Decode a message handed out by pool room helpers	Desktop systems
5	Register on the UBSY website and complete a Sudoku	Students' union
6	Spot clues hidden in the fire safety video	Health and safety
7	Reflect on their first terms study in the Good Study Guide blog	Good study guide
8	Find information placed in the "Look After Yourself" section of student services and on posters	Student services
9	View a video and collaborate to take photos and load on community	Learning technologies
10	Debriefing, main prize distribution, evaluation	

Note: Replicated from "Using alternate reality games to support first year induction with ELGG," Piatt, K., 2009, *Campus-Wide Information Systems*. Copyright 2009 by Emerald

ter. While the students were conducting each quest, they obtained useful information for their campus lives. Table 10.1 shows the activities for the game (Piatt, 2009).

Students who participated in this game experience discovery, exploration, and competition. They also may feel "part of something special" which can contribute to retention. "Who is Herring Hale?" was a good attempt to help new students become familiar with the new and strange environment of the university. Students sometimes have difficulty in studying and living because of lack of necessary information rather than insufficient environment and knowledge. It can be used for not only higher educational institutes, but also K-12 schools. For example, orientations for K-12 students and their parents can be a smaller version of "Who is Herring Hale?"

10.3 Star Question

Star Question was developed to help undergraduate students review what they learned in class (Kim, 2014). When the final examination was near, some students showed the following behaviors:

- Cram for the exams of relatively easy courses
- Lose chances to ask questions to lecturers
- Do not recognize their progresses

To solve these problems, Star Question includes the following goals (Kim, 2014).

- Have a review time in the class
- Provide immediate feedback
- Have students to share important concepts with other classmates

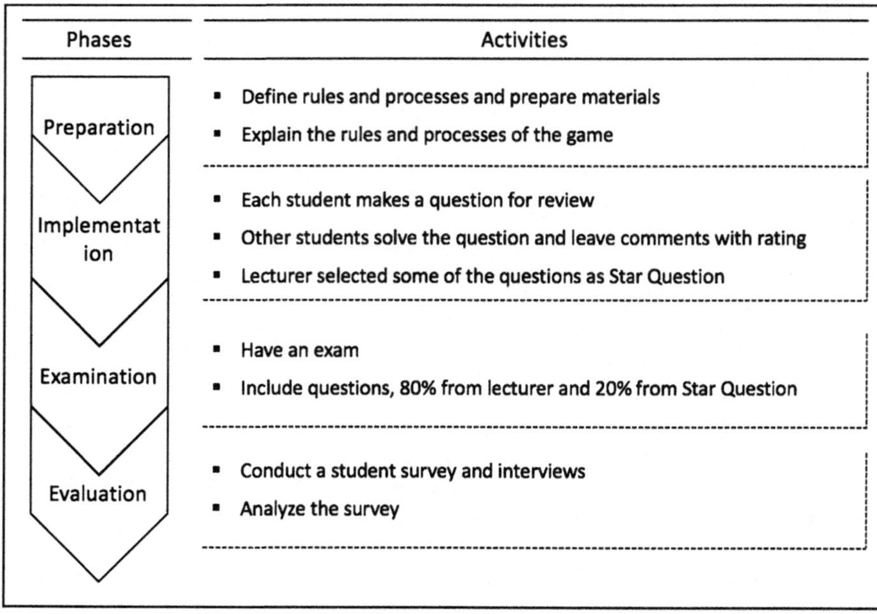

Fig. 10.2 Phases and activities of Star Question

Star Question employs rating, commenting, and badge systems. Figure 10.2 illustrates the phases and activities of Star Question.

Students receive badges when their questions are chosen to be used for Star Question. The lecturer also includes student names in the exam paper to show the copyright. If a question is to be included in another examination in the future, the name of the student who created the question will always be included in the exam paper with the copyright mark.

After the examination, the lecturer conducts a survey to ascertain the effectiveness of Star Question and interviews students to discuss their experiences during the gamified review process.

Students who participated in Star Question agreed that it was helpful to experience increased levels of understanding, to review what they had learned in the class, and to reduce stress from reviewing the lessons and preparing for the examination.

10.4 Multiplayer Classroom

Sheldon (2012) designed the multiplayer classroom for Theory & Practice of Game Design course at Indiana University, Bloomington. Each class consists of three tasks (see Table 10.2).

Table 10.2 Tasks in multiplayer classroom

Task	Activity
Fighting monsters	Quiz and exam
Completing quests	Presentations of games and research
Crafting	Personal game premises, game analysis papers, and video game concept document

The grading system for the class is based on the game level and experience point. Students need to accumulate experience points to reach a specific game level. The final game level becomes the grade at the end of the semester.

Students can attain experience points by conducting individual and group activities. The group in the class is called a guild. Students can create a guild based on common interests and ideas. Each guild takes a zone in the classroom and collaborates to achieve the goals of the guild. There are six zones:

- Ocean of immersion
- Empathy acres
- Feedback farms
- Wandering wastes
- Interface island
- The verbal vale

The guild does not stay at one zone. Each guild rotates from zone to zone during the semester. This is for preventing slack attitudes.

This gamified class uses avatar, game level, experience point, guild, quest, and combat as mechanics. Sheldon's design for this class is a meaningful attempt to promote student engagement and collaboration skills.

10.5 Classcraft

Shawn Young, a Canadian high school teacher, developed Classcraft (Classcraft Studio Inc., 2016) to facilitate desired behaviors, such as student engagement and collaboration, through a role-playing game. Classcraft has been used at K-12 schools and higher educational institutions in many countries.

Students in a class using Classcraft (Classcraft Studio Inc., 2016) can choose their game characters, such as Mages, Warriors, and Healers. Each game character has a different amount of health points and action points. There are five types of points: health points, action points, experience points, gold pieces, and power points (see Table 10.3).

Teachers can adjust each point depending on their needs. Table 10.4 shows an example of point settings in Classcraft (Classcraft Studio Inc., 2016).

The teacher can use different point policies depending on game characters. For example, the teacher can allow students who choose Mage to be late for the class up to 2 min. The teacher can add fun to the class by using different policies like this.

Table 10.3 Point types in Classcraft

Point	Description
Health points (HP)	Character's life energy
Experience points (XP)	Students earn XP when they demonstrate desired behaviors. The teacher can input the desired behaviors
Action points (AP)	Students spend AP when they use their powers
Gold pieces (GP)	Students earn GP when the teacher recognizes a student's extra efforts and contributions Students can use GP for customizing their characters
Power points (PP)	Students earn PP when they level up. Students can use PP for learning new powers

Table 10.4 Examples of point configuration in Classcraft

Point type	Behavior	Point
XP	Finds mistakes in learning material	50
	Achieves at least 70% on a test	30
	Answers questions in class	60
	Helps other students	75
	Enthusiastically participates in class activities	100
HP	Late for class	−10
	Interrupts class	−5
	Submits incomplete assignments	−10
	Does not participate in class activities	−20
	Achieves less than 60% on a test	−5
PP	Helps other students with own PP	5

Also, this approach can be a useful means to help students who have special needs. For example, some students have insufficient time to come to the class because of their schedule. They can avoid tardiness by using the special ability of a Mage. Teachers should analyze students' needs and wants for deciding the special abilities of each game character. Without analyzing them, it is difficult to determine the appropriate game characters and abilities. Also, students may not be interested in selecting and using a game character.

With Classcraft (Classcraft Studio Inc., 2016), teachers can observe and analyze students' behaviors using analytics feature. They can track positive and negative behaviors of students. The information provided by the analytics feature can be used for improving the current class and also for designing future classes.

10.6 simSchool

simSchool (2005) is a classroom simulator for teachers and prospective teachers. It provides them with an environment where they can learn important concepts for understanding their students and making effective classes. Many educators and researchers from different countries have used simSchool as a simulation tool, research sandbox, or intervention tool (Willis et al., 2017).

In simSchool (2005), teachers can create a virtual class with diverse students in terms of ethnicity, gender, language proficiency, and range of special needs. They can take actions to teach the students and immediately see students' reactions.

While playing with the plan-do-check-adjust (PDCA) method-based simulation for continual improvement of the class, teachers can enhance their knowledge of student need analysis, differentiation of instruction, student outcomes, and application of the outcomes. Also, prospective teachers can increase their self-efficacy and self-confidence.

References

Classcraft Studio Inc. (2016). *Classcraft*. Available from https://www.classcraft.com

Just Press Play. (2012). *Just Press Play*. Available from http://www.justpressplayonline.com

Kim, S. (2014). Gamification of a reviewing process using self-setting question and game mechanism in undergraduate education. *World Applied Sciences Journal*, *30*(11), 1605–1609.

Piatt, K. (2009). Using alternate reality games to support first year induction with ELGG. *Campus-Wide Information Systems*, *26*(4), 313–322.

simSchool. (2005). *simSchool*. Available from http://www.simschool.org

Sheldon, L. (2012). *The multiplayer classroom: Designing coursework as a game*. Boston, MA: Course Technology PTR.

Werbach, K., & Hunter, D. (2012). *For the win: How game thinking can revolutionize your business*. Philadelphia, PA: Wharton Digital Press.

Willis, J., Greenhalgh, S., Nadolny, L., Liu, S., Aldemir, T., Rogers, S., … Oliver, W. (2017). Exploring the rules of the game: Games in the classroom, game-based learning, gamification, and simulations. In P. Resta & S. Smith (Eds.), *Proceedings of Society for Information Technology & Teacher Education International Conference 2017* (pp. 475–480). Chesapeake, VA: Association for the Advancement of Computing in Education (AACE).

Chapter 11
Gamification Cases in STEM Education

Quest
Let's explore gamification cases in science and engineering education.
Let's figure out how each case can be used for your STEM education.

11.1 Labster

Labster (2011) is an educational simulation that provides learners with virtual laboratory environments for biology, chemistry, and general science investigations. Since it has game-like graphics and scenarios, learners, especially young learners, can be more interested in the lab simulation and science learning.

In Labster, a learner can choose a laboratory from the category list (see Table 11.1). Since Labster's immersive 3D graphics illustrate real laboratory environments, learners can easily understand the characteristics of each laboratory and learning content. They also learn how students as researchers conduct experiments in each laboratory, such as designing experiments, manipulating data, analyzing results, and arriving at conclusions. Table 11.1 shows the list of laboratories of Labster.

Figure 11.1 illustrates the Enzyme Kinetics Lab in Labster. Learners can experience the lab environment and conduct research using the experiment equipment and materials in the simulated lab. They can learn what they need to do in the lab for conducting research and choose various options of exploring possible scenarios in the lab.

Figure 11.2 describes the experiment data given to a learner. The learner analyzes the data and sees the experiment results. Through this process, the learners using Labster can understand the characteristics of the materials that were used for an experiment and the differences caused by diverse experiment scenarios.

Unlike the traditional science classrooms using textbooks and the laboratories that allow only limited experiments with predefined scenarios, the simulation that

S. Kim et al., *Gamification in Learning and Education*, Advances in Game-Based Learning, DOI 10.1007/978-3-319-47283-6_11

Table 11.1 Laboratories of Labster (2011)

Category	Lab
Biochemistry	Antibodies, carbohydrates, cellular respiration, crime scene investigation, enzyme kinetics, fermentation, introduction to food macromolecule, introductory lab, photosynthesis, plant transcriptomics, protein synthesis
Biotechnology	Biological circuit, FACS, genetically engineered machine, MAGE, molecular cloning, next-generation sequencing, synthetic biology, tissue engineering
Cellular and molecular biology	Cell culture basics, gene expression, gene regulation, mammalian transient protein expression, meiosis, microscopy, mitosis, pluripotent stem cell culture
Ecology	Eutrophication, marine biology
Evolution and life diversity	Evolution
Genetics	Animal genetics, cytogenetics, medical genetics, Mendelian inheritance, monogenetic disorders
Microbiology	Bacterial isolation
Analytical chemistry	Flow injection analysis, HPLC, nuclear magnetic resonance, titration
General chemistry	Acids and bases, chemistry safety, ionic and covalent bonds
Lab basics	Lab safety

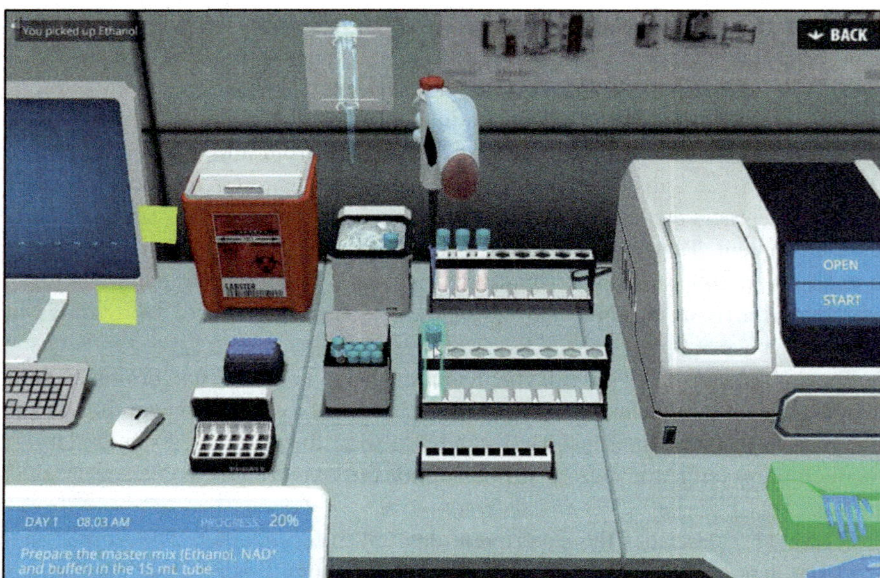

Fig. 11.1 Enzyme Kinetics Lab in Labster (Reproduced from Labster website, 2017, Retrieved from www.labster.com Copyright 2017 by Labster)

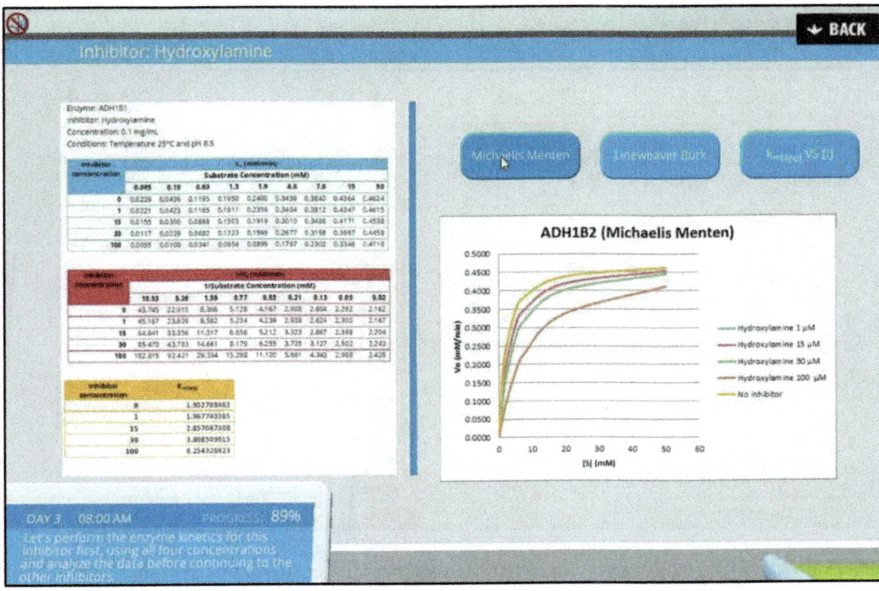

Fig. 11.2 Data analysis in the Enzyme Kinetics Lab (Reproduced from Labster website, 2017, Retrieved from www.labster.com Copyright 2017 by Labster)

intrinsically embeds learners' participation and allows various attempts can promote engagement and provide a chance to test the individual learner's hypotheses or theories. This approach can strengthen learners' knowledge organization.

11.2 CodeCombat

CodeCombat (2016) is a website that offers programming learning environments using a role-playing game. A learner creates a game character to begin programming learning. While playing a game, the learner must write codes to conduct tasks and achieve goals. As the learner successfully completes each task, the learner receives experience points and gems that present the progress of learning. The teacher can set up a class in CodeCombat to see the progress of each learner. The programming languages supported by CodeCombat include Python, JavaScript, CoffeeScript, and Lua. Learners can learn programming elements, such as syntax, methods, parameters, strings, loops, arguments, variables, and operators. Many educators at K-12 schools choose Python and JavaScript as a primary programming language for their classes. Figure 11.3 illustrates a CodeCombat game in which a learner can control the game character to complete a mission by running the code the learner creates. In Fig. 11.3, the learner used various programming elements, such as parameters, variables, loops, and conditional statements.

Fig. 11.3 A CodeCombat game controlled by a learner's code (Reproduced from CodeCombat website, 2016, Retrieved from https://codecombat.com Copyright 2016 by CodeCombat)

CodeCombat employs various game elements. The progress and achievement of a learner affects the damage level, health, speed, and weapons of the game character. Learners may also form a clan to pursue a common goal. If a learner completes a level, the next level will be unlocked. The game character uses equipment, weapons, and other game items. Figure 11.4 illustrates CodeCombat's game characters. Each game character has different abilities, and a learner can choose a character based on their preferences. For example, if a learner prefers a speedy character, the learner will compare the speed level of each game character to choose the fastest character. Figure 11.4 also shows some locked game characters. As a game element, unlocking can be used for gamification. Learners can feel a sense of accomplishment by unlocking the locked game characters.

Figure 11.5 describes some of the game elements in CodeCombat, which are levels, points, virtual currency, missions, and rewards. As a learner completes missions at each level, the learner receives rewards including experience points and virtual currency. As seen in Fig. 11.5, the experience point of each level is not the same. Also, the reward amount of a higher level is not always more than the one of a lower level in order to provide a reasonable reward system. If an instructor wants to use the level, virtual currency, and points as criteria for grading, he or she should listen to learners' opinions on the reward system through a pilot test.

11.3 Plantville

Plantville (Johnson & Respini-Irwin, 2011; Siemens, 2011) is a simulation game developed by Siemens to help new employees and prospective employees understand industrial plant management and technologies. Since the plant business is one

Fig. 11.4 Game characters in CodeCombat (Reproduced from CodeCombat website, 2016, Retrieved from https://codecombat.com Copyright 2016 by CodeCombat)

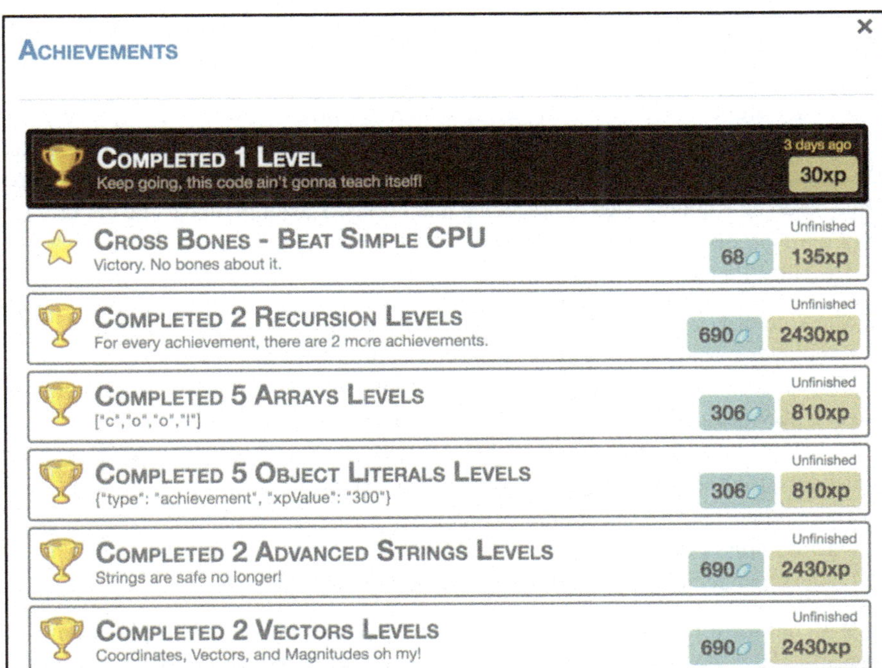

Fig. 11.5 Game levels and points in CodeCombat (Reproduced from CodeCombat website, 2016, Retrieved from https://codecombat.com Copyright 2016 by CodeCombat)

of the core business sectors of Siemens, and most new and prospective employees have insufficient experience in a plant business, it is required to provide them with an environment that deepens their knowledge on the plant business.

The learners can enhance their understanding of the plant business by building and operating a plant within the game. They explore the roles and various experiences of a plant manager. Also, given the conditions, they try to find optimal solutions to achieve higher productivity, efficiency, and sustainability.

Siemens opened this simulation game to the public for another purpose which is to improve its brand power and engage customers and potential customers. As a result, more people might understand not only the plant business, but also the technologies of Siemens. Additionally, Siemens expects that Plantville (Johnson & Respini-Irwin, 2011; Siemens, 2011) can motivate talented people from a variety of countries to apply for employment.

11.4 Kumon

Kumon (2015) is one of the largest private after-school tutoring organizations in the world. It shares ideas on how to gamify mathematics learning via its website (http://www.kumon.com/resources/). Although its focus is not classroom teaching, it provides educators and parents with simple and practical gamification methods.

The gamification ideas that Kumon (2015) shares use toys, household items, edible foods, or traditional children's games. For example, the hopscotch game can be used for learning mathematics by replacing the number in each section with a mathematics question and solving the question to move forward (see Fig. 11.6).

Another example is to use a jump rope game. Kumon suggests that a jump rope game can be used for learning counting and adding numbers. Figure 11.7 illustrates a jump rope game based on Kumon's idea of practicing math skills. The jump rope game in Fig. 11.7 is for third through sixth graders to practice addition, multiplication, and squaring.

The rules for the jump rope game in Fig. 11.7 are:

- The winner is the player who reaches 1,000 or higher score first.
- If a player reaches 100 or more, the player multiplies the score by two.
- If a player reaches 150 or more, the player adds the squared number of the difference between the two players' numbers of jumps at this round.
- If a player reaches 200 or more, the player receives a magic card which can be used to stop the game and play Minecraft for 30 min.
- The winner receives one diamond point.
- One diamond point can be exchanged with one dollar.
- Players can decide when and how to use the diamond point.

With the gamified jump rope, a learner can practice addition, multiplication, and squaring. Other mathematical concepts can be included in the game as well depending on the needs of the learners. For example, subtraction, division, exponent, or other more complicate concepts can be added to the game for higher grades.

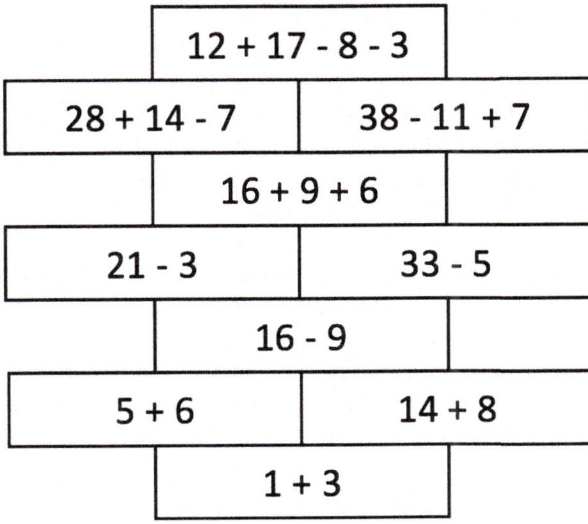

Fig. 11.6 Hopscotch game for learning addition and subtraction

Dad	Dad Score	Tim	Tim Score	Rewards
57	57	76	76	
81	138	103	179 -> 358	Multiply Tim' score by two
123	261 -> 522	91	449	Multiply dad' score by two
130	652	151	600 -> 1041	Square difference

Winner : Tim

Fig 11.7 A gamified jump rope for learning mathematics

11.5 Stop Disasters

The United Nations (UN) and the International Strategy for Disaster Reduction (ISDR), which is an organizational unit of the UN for supporting disaster reduction activities, provide a free online simulation game, named Stop Disasters (Playerthree & UN/ISDR, 2007), in which learners can experience the issues associated with natural disasters. In this simulation game, given a limited budget, learners can manipulate various variables, such as residential building types, defensive construction types, training methods, or disaster prevention and emergency equipment types. Figures 11.8 and 11.9 illustrate situations in which a player develops land and constructs defenses against natural disasters.

A player in the game can run a disaster simulation after developing land and installing defensive construction and equipment. The player can then observe situations caused by a natural disaster through an animation reflecting possible situations. Also, the player receives a report describing the result of the simulation. Figure 11.10 illustrates the report.

Players who successfully complete a mission receive a medal (see Fig. 11.11) and have a chance to add their name to a leaderboard, called the high-score chart in this game. Figure 11.12 illustrates the leaderboard. It is a micro leaderboard rather than macro leaderboard. If a player selects a disaster scenario among tsunami, hurricane, wild fire, earthquake, and flood, a micro leaderboard associated with the selected scenario appears. Also, the level of difficulty is another criterion for categorizing micro leaderboards.

With Stop Disasters, students can see what activities are more effective than others to minimize the damages from each natural disaster. This simulation game is similar to SimCity, an urban planning simulation game developed by Electronic Arts, but reflects more realistic disasters. Thus, students can learn lessons that can be more meaningful for the real world.

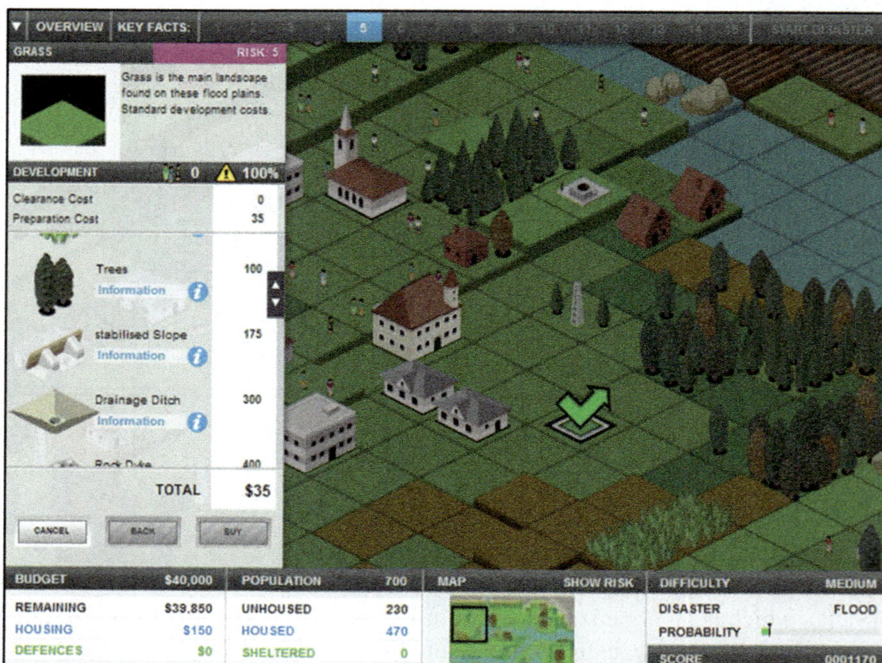

Fig. 11.8. Land development in Stop Disasters (Reproduced from Stop Disasters website, 2017, Retrieved from http://www.stopdisastersgame.org Copyright 2017 by Playerthree and UN/ISDR) (Note: Playerthree developed Stop Disasters for the UN/ISDR)

Fig. 11.9 Disaster prevention activity in Stop Disasters (Reproduced from Stop Disasters website, 2017, Retrieved from http://www.stopdisastersgame.org Copyright 2017 by Playerthree and UN/ISDR)

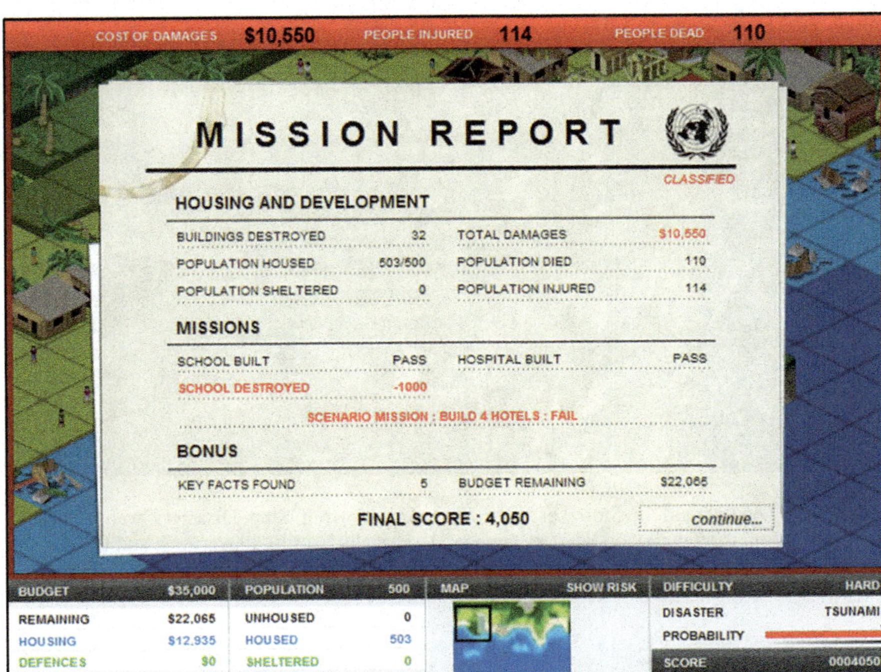

Fig. 11.10 Mission report in Stop Disasters (Reproduced from Stop Disasters website, 2017, Retrieved from http://www.stopdisastersgame.org Copyright 2017 by Playerthree and UN/ISDR)

Fig. 11.11 Medal in Stop Disasters (Reproduced from Stop Disasters website, 2017, Retrieved from http://www.stopdisastersgame.org Copyright 2017 by Playerthree and UN/ISDR)

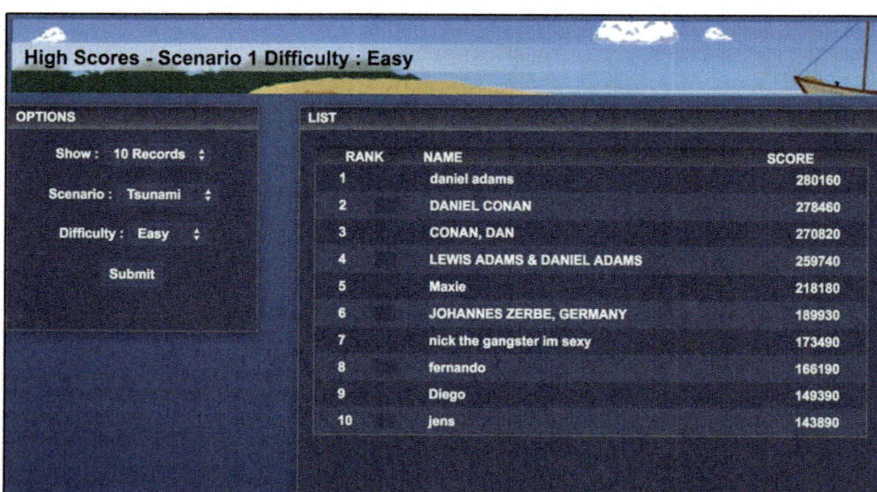

Fig. 11.12 Leaderboard in Stop Disasters (Reproduced from Stop Disasters website, 2017, Retrieved from http://www.stopdisastersgame.org Copyright 2017 by Playerthree and UN/ISDR)

11.6 The Radix Endeavor

The Radix Endeavor (Massachusetts Institute of Technology, 2013) is a massively multiplayer online game. It was developed by Education Arcade and Scheller Teacher Education Program at Massachusetts Institute of Technology (MIT) with a grant from the Bill and Melinda Gates Foundation. It was designed for middle and high schoolers learning algebra, geometry, probability, statistics, ecology, evolution, genetics, and the systems of human body.

The Radix Endeavor has narratives and graphic designs that can be found in conventional games to encourage students' perceptions of the learning process as being fun, and not a boring or forced activity. Players can decide the look of their own game characters (see Fig. 11.13) and take actions by intention and planning.

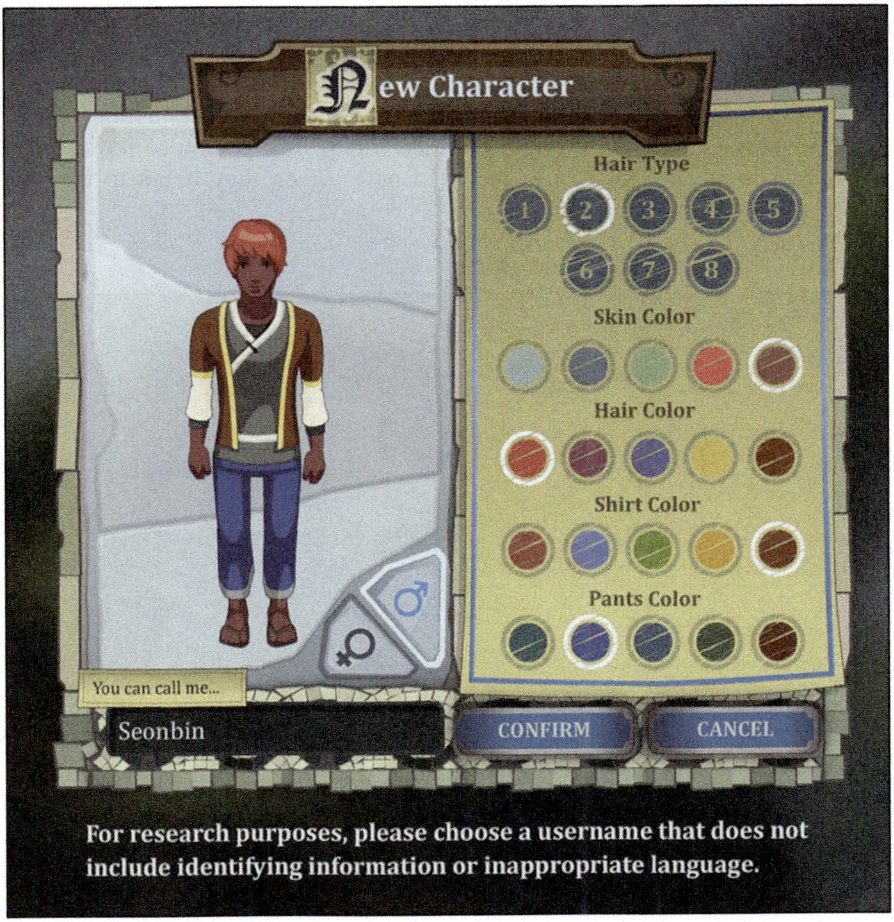

Fig. 11.13 Game character design in The Radix Endeavor (Reproduced from The Radix Endeavor website, 2017, Retrieved from https://www.radixendeavor.org Copyright 2017 by Massachusetts Institute of Technology (MIT))

Some players who have been passive in classrooms become very active in this learning process and try to find information necessary for solving a problem even without any instruction. The Radix Endeavor is an example of a learning environment where students can experience self-directed learning.

In addition to self-directed learning, players can experience collaborative learning by cooperating with other players for conducting quests. The Radix Endeavor asks players to complete various quests. Some of the quests are not easy to complete alone. The collaboration is a useful means to successfully complete the difficult quests. A player can check on a required quest via a standing bulletin board and available resources for conducting the quest via the inventory menu (see Fig. 11.14).

In the reputation menu, players can see their progress by topics in each subject (see Fig. 11.15). Also, they can see quest logs presenting a list of completed quests and in-progress quests (see Fig. 11.16).

Figure 11.17 illustrates a field note in the game. This feature can be useful for students who want to record important information, review activities beyond quest logs, and plan activities. Unlike The Radix Endeavor, some games developed for STEM education do not include the note-taking feature. Because taking notes can improve learning, it may be a good idea for teachers to suggest their students to use the field notes when they begin to use this game.

Fig. 11.14 Quest in The Radix Endeavor (Reproduced from The Radix Endeavor website, 2017, Retrieved from https://www.radixendeavor.org Copyright 2017 by Massachusetts Institute of Technology (MIT))

Fig. 11.15 Reputation in The Radix Endeavor (Reproduced from The Radix Endeavor website, 2017, Retrieved from https://www.radixendeavor.org Copyright 2017 by Massachusetts Institute of Technology (MIT))

The Radix Endeavor is a useful game to help students learn problem-solving skills, as well as topics in biology and mathematics. At the same time, it can be one of the best places for teachers who are interested in engagement, motivation, self-directed learning, and collaborative learning through gamification. The teachers can explore how their students can learn in the game. Also, teachers can monitor students' activities and support them if needed. Teachers can also manage classrooms and students with the teacher module.

Fig. 11.16 Quest log in The Radix Endeavor (Reproduced from The Radix Endeavor website, 2017, Retrieved from https://www.radixendeavor.org Copyright 2017 by Massachusetts Institute of Technology (MIT))

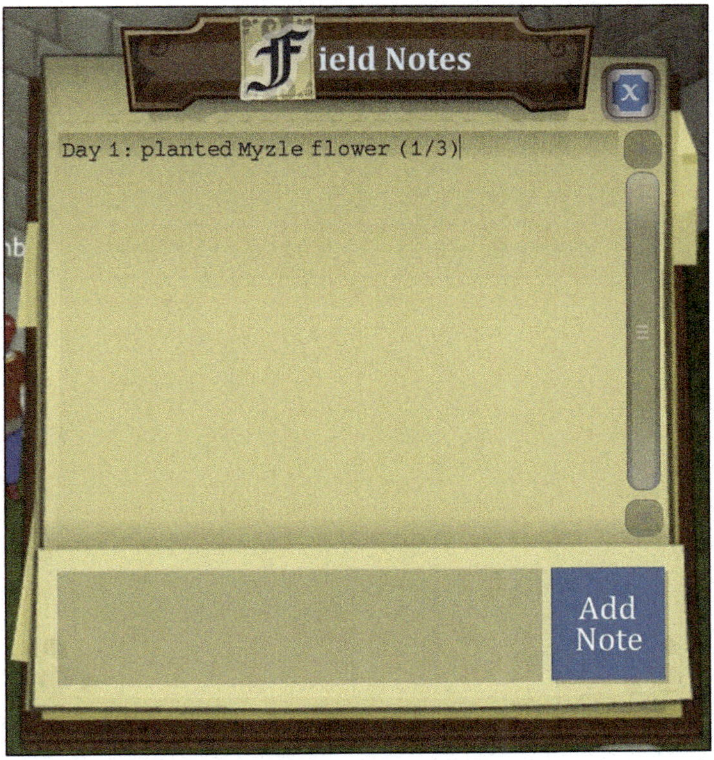

Fig. 11.17 Field notes in The Radix Endeavor (Reproduced from The Radix Endeavor website, 2017, Retrieved from https://www.radixendeavor.org Copyright 2017 by Massachusetts Institute of Technology (MIT))

References

CodeCombat. (2016). *CodeCombat*. Available from https://codecombat.com

Johnson, N. S., & Respini-Irwin, C. (2011). Move over, FarmVille: Siemens launches Plantville game. *Cadalyst, 28*(1), 8. Retrieved from http://login.ezproxy.lib.vt.edu/login?url=http://search.proquest.com.ezproxy.lib.vt.edu/docview/1704185074?accountid=14826

Kumon. (2015). *Study tips & resources*. Retrieved from https://www.kumon.com

Labster. (2011). *Labster*. Available from www.labster.com

Massachusetts Institute of Technology. (2013). *The Radix Endeavor*. Available from https://www.radixendeavor.org

Playerthree & UN/ISDR. (2007). *Stop disasters*. Available from http://www.stopdisastersgame.org

Siemens. (2011). *Siemens launches Plantville*. Retrieved from https://www.siemens.ca

Chapter 12
Gamification Cases in Liberal Arts and Social Science Education

Quest
Let's explore gamification cases in liberal arts and social science education.
Let's figure out how each case can be used as models to enhance learning in liberal arts and social science settings.

12.1 Duolingo

Duolingo (2011) is one of the largest language-learning platforms where learners can learn various foreign languages, including Spanish, French, German, Italian, Portuguese, Russian, Dutch, Swedish, Irish, Turkish, Danish, Norwegian, Polish, Esperanto, Hebrew, Ukrainian, Vietnamese, Welsh, Hungarian, Greek, and Romanian. It started as a spin-off from the School of Computer Science at Carnegie Mellon University and has been selected as one of the best app by Apple (iPhone App of the Year) and Google (Best of the Best for Android).

For motivating and engaging learners, Duolingo (2011) uses multiple game mechanics, such as experience points, virtual currency, leaderboards, and unlocking. Figure 12.1 illustrates experience points (XP) in Duolingo. Learners can see daily XP and accumulated XP.

Learners need to complete missions to increase their XPs. Successful completion of a test is one of the missions. Figure 12.2 shows a question for the test. In the case of Fig. 12.2, the learner has to correctly read and speak the French sentence presented on the screen to increase the XP.

Duolingo (2011) uses Lingots as its virtual currency which can be earned by studying lessons for 10 days on a streak, finishing a lesson, finishing a new skill, and inviting friends. Figure 12.3 illustrates the Lingot store where learners can use Lingots to acquire special game items.

S. Kim et al., *Gamification in Learning and Education*, Advances in Game-Based Learning, DOI 10.1007/978-3-319-47283-6_12

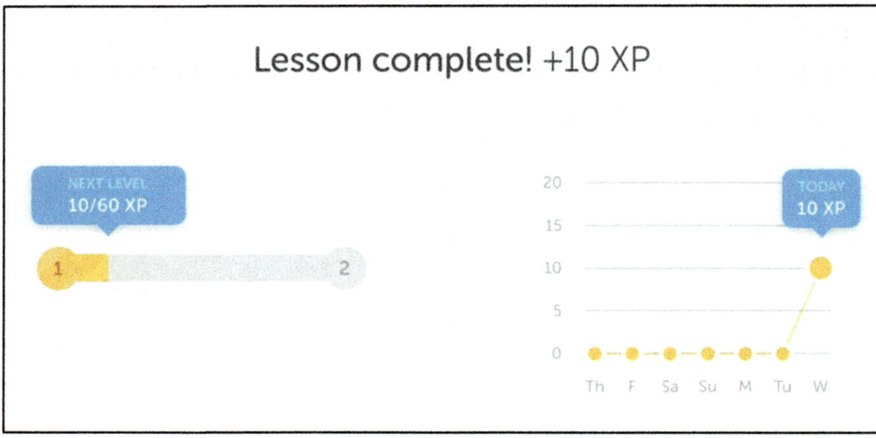

Fig. 12.1 Experience points in Duolingo (Reproduced from Duolingo website, 2017, Retrieved from www.duolingo.com Copyright 2017 by Duolingo)

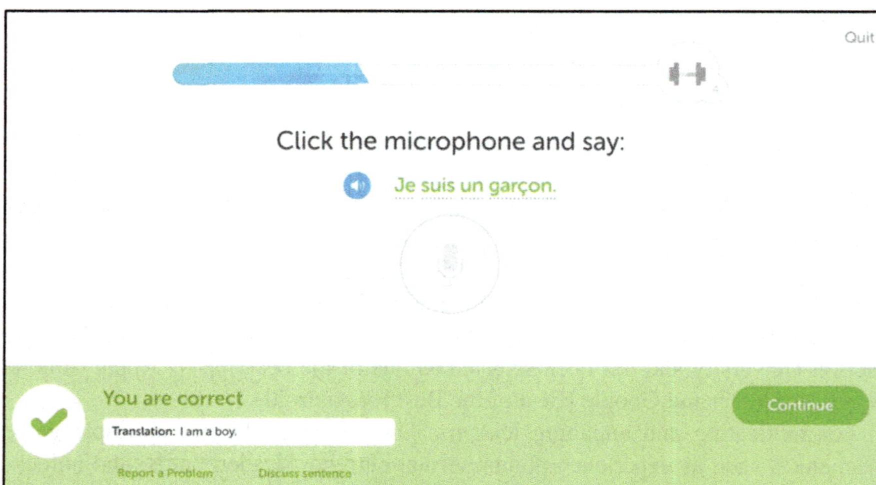

Fig. 12.2 Speaking test in Duolingo (Reproduced from Duolingo website, 2017, Retrieved from www.duolingo.com Copyright 2017 by Duolingo)

Duolingo (2011) allows only those who completed the previous lesson to take the next lesson. Figure 12.4 shows that the learner who completed lesson 1 can redo lesson 1 or begin lesson 2 but not lesson 3.

In addition to the game mechanics described above, Duolingo (2011) uses hearts which is similar to the health level of a game character in a role-playing or action game. If a learner makes a mistake in lessons, practices, or tests, the learner loses a heart. If a learner without any hearts makes another mistake, the learner fails the lesson, practice, or test.

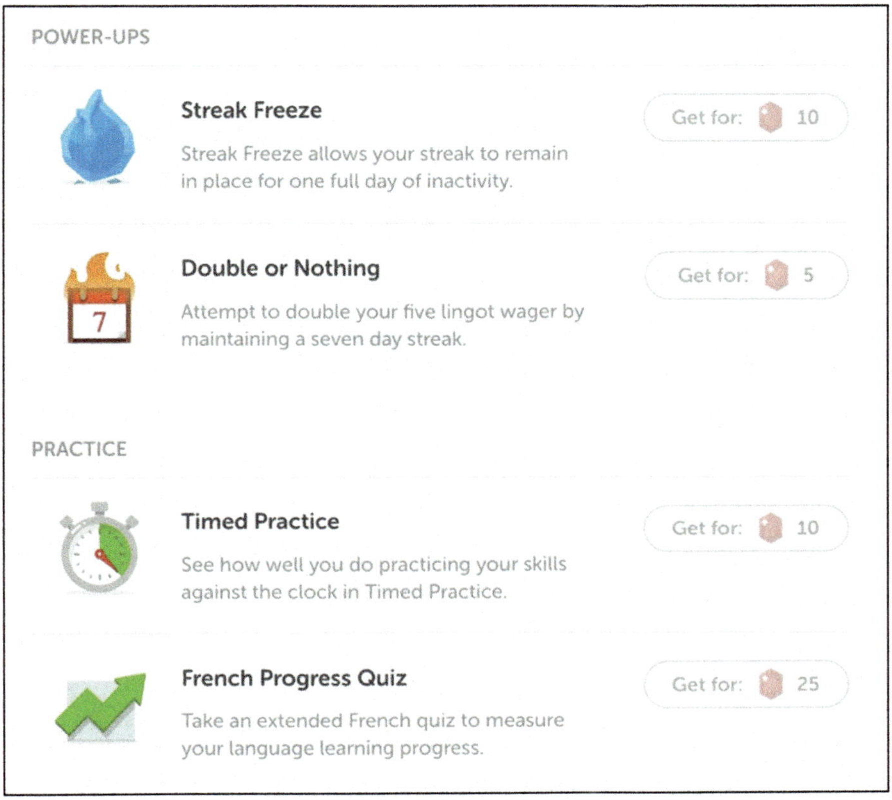

Fig. 12.3 Virtual currency named Lingot in Duolingo (Reproduced from Duolingo website, 2017 Retrieved from www.duolingo.com Copyright 2017 by Duolingo)

Learners from many countries are using Duolingo (2011) for learning foreign languages. Although some of them say the content of Duolingo is not practical and rarely use the game expressions in the real world, many learners agree that Duolingo is one of the best places to begin learning a foreign language due to its gamified learning and interactivity.

12.2 Practice Series

McGraw-Hill Education (2012) has produced educational 3D multiplayer games, called Practice Series, covering various disciplines including politics, marketing, and foreign languages. Some high schools and colleges have used the Practice Series to engage students in learning subject matter from those disciplines.

Practice Government (McGraw-Hill Education, 2012) is one of the Practice Series games where students play as members of the US Congress. While playing

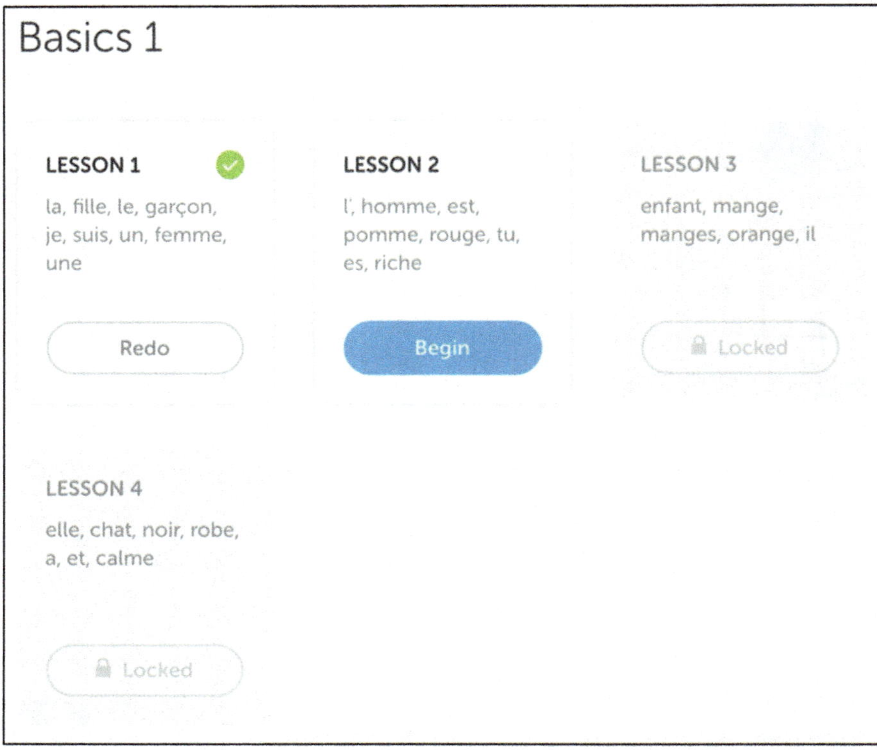

Fig. 12.4 Unlocking in Duolingo (Reproduced from Duolingo website, 2017, Retrieved from www.duolingo.com Copyright 2017 by Duolingo)

the game, students can learn political systems of the USA. The mission in this game is to maximize political capital by creating legislation and taking political actions such as media campaigns.

As another Practice Series game, Practice Marketing (McGraw-Hill Education, 2012) has been introduced to educational game markets. It is a business strategy game in which students learn marketing strategies and practice them in a backpack market. The students act as marketing managers and use information obtained in the game on competitors and the feedback from executives. Also, they make decisions necessary for successful businesses. For example, they decide the features, shapes, materials, and straps of backpacks.

Practice Spanish (McGraw-Hill Education, 2012), one of the Practice Series, is another good case of gamification in learning and education. It is a Spanish-learning game that consists of 13 quests. Students can learn verbal expressions used in daily life while they are carrying out each quest in a fictional Columbian town. Also, by playing mini-games before conducting each quest, students can learn vocabulary and grammar that will be needed to successfully complete the quest. This game includes some exciting stories, such as handling ghosts and robberies, to engage students in the game.

12.3 Economics Games

Nicolas Gruyer and Nicolas Toublanc have developed Economics Games (Gruyer & Toublanc, 2012), which have been used for education at Agro Paris Tech, Ecole des Ponts Paris Tech, Harvard University, Toulouse Business School, and others. The simulation games cover topics in environmental economics, energy economics, industrial organization, microeconomics, and other economics and business administration areas.

AirECONsim (Gruyer & Toublanc, 2012) is one of the simulation games with educational purposes that Economics Games has developed. It is an airline simulation game where learners can learn industrial organization and microeconomics by playing the game as a fleet and pricing policy manager at an airline. The goal of the game is to maximize the profit of the airline. For achieving the goal, a player needs to consider market, competitor, regulation, new aircraft, new route, traffic, and other conditions.

The player begins the game with a simple price plan, but as the player makes progress, more rules and conditions are given. Figure 12.5 illustrates the simplest pricing plan used at the beginning of the game. The player decides the price for a seat with the purpose of making the biggest profit. On the other hand, Fig. 12.6 shows a little bit more complicated pricing plan. At this phase, the player needs to decide a quota, the number of seats, that will be sold at a specific price and another price for the seats beyond the quota.

Figure 12.7 describes more conditions, the number of round trips for peak and off-peak periods and the aircraft size. The player experiences more and more conditions while moving to higher levels.

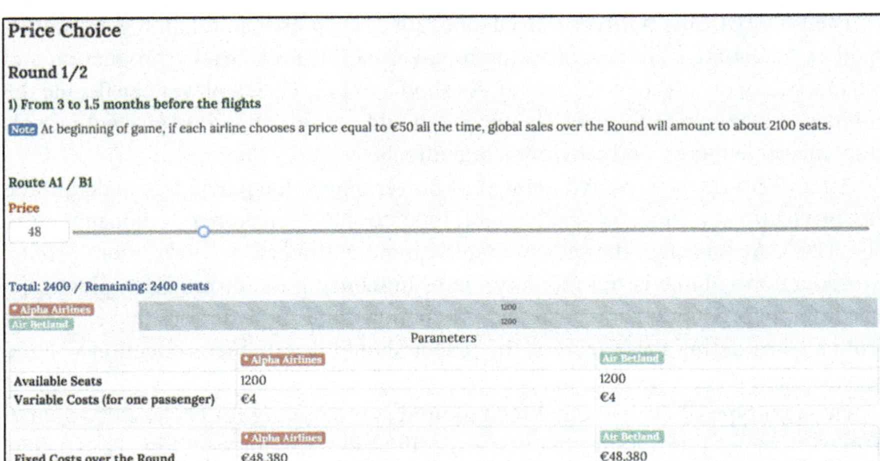

Fig. 12.5 Simple airfare pricing in AirECONsim (Reproduced from lud.io website, 2017 Retrieved from https://lud.io Copyright 2017 by Economics Games, Nicolas Gruyer, and Nicolas Toublanc)

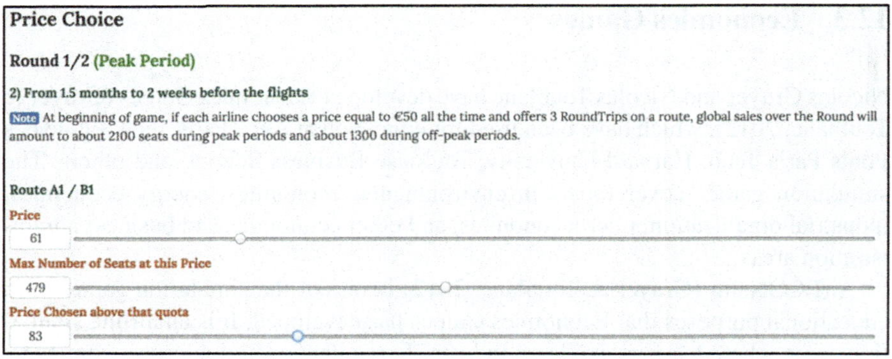

Fig. 12.6 Advanced airfare pricing in AirECONsim (Reproduced from lud.io website, 2017, Retrieved from https://lud.io Copyright 2017 by Economics Games, Nicolas Gruyer, and Nicolas Toublanc)

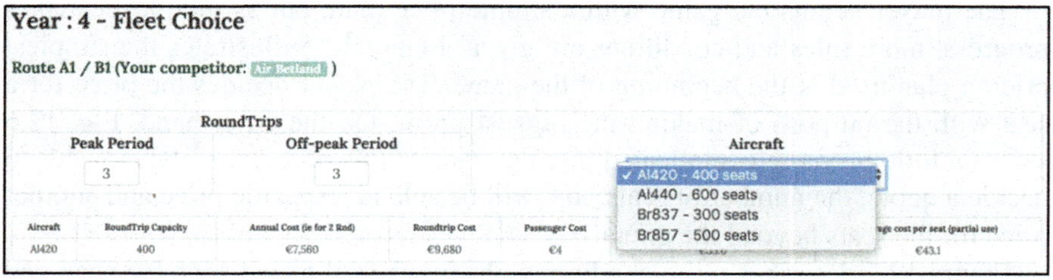

Fig. 12.7 Fleet choice in AirECONsim (Reproduced from lud.io website, 2017, Retrieved from https://lud.io Copyright 2017 by Economics Games, Nicolas Gruyer, and Nicolas Toublanc)

The Energy Game (Gruyer & Toublanc, 2012) is another simulation game developed by Economics Games, in which a player can plan electricity production and sell electricity on a wholesale market. As shown in Fig. 12.8, a player can decide the number of plants in each type. The player should consider possible production volume, investment cost, and environmental effects.

After deciding the type and number of power plants, the player has to determine the production volume of each plant type to meet customers' demands (see Fig. 12.9). At this step, the player should be more strategic to make more profits. A production volume is not the only factor influencing the profit. Each plant type has different production unit costs and production unit CO_2 emissions that can affect profits. Considering these factors, the player should decide the production volume of each plant type.

The next type of decision making required is the pricing for each sales volume. A player can set a different price for a specific sales volume (see Fig. 12.10). The player should estimate the possible sales volume and decide the unit price for each sales volume for maximizing the profit from selling electricity.

Now, the player can see the business outcomes. Figure 12.11 illustrates the results that include sales volume, revenue, fixed cost, production cost, profit, and

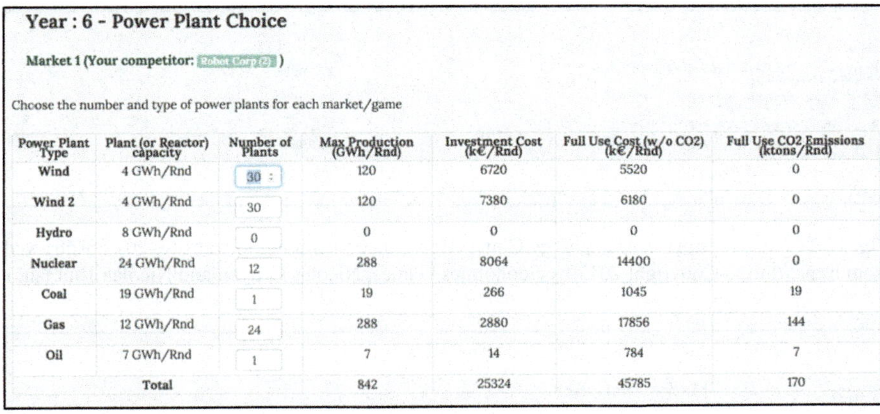

Year : 6 - Power Plant Choice

Market 1 (Your competitor: Robot Corp (2))

Choose the number and type of power plants for each market/game

Power Plant Type	Plant (or Reactor) capacity	Number of Plants	Max Production (GWh/Rnd)	Investment Cost (k€/Rnd)	Full Use Cost (w/o CO2) (k€/Rnd)	Full Use CO2 Emissions (ktons/Rnd)
Wind	4 GWh/Rnd	30	120	6720	5520	0
Wind 2	4 GWh/Rnd	30	120	7380	6180	0
Hydro	8 GWh/Rnd	0	0	0	0	0
Nuclear	24 GWh/Rnd	12	288	8064	14400	0
Coal	19 GWh/Rnd	1	19	266	1045	19
Gas	12 GWh/Rnd	24	288	2880	17856	144
Oil	7 GWh/Rnd	1	7	14	784	7
	Total		842	25324	45785	170

Fig. 12.8 Power plant choice in The Energy Game (Reproduced from lud.io website, 2017, Retrieved from https://lud.io Copyright 2017 by Economics Games, Nicolas Gruyer, and Nicolas Toublanc)

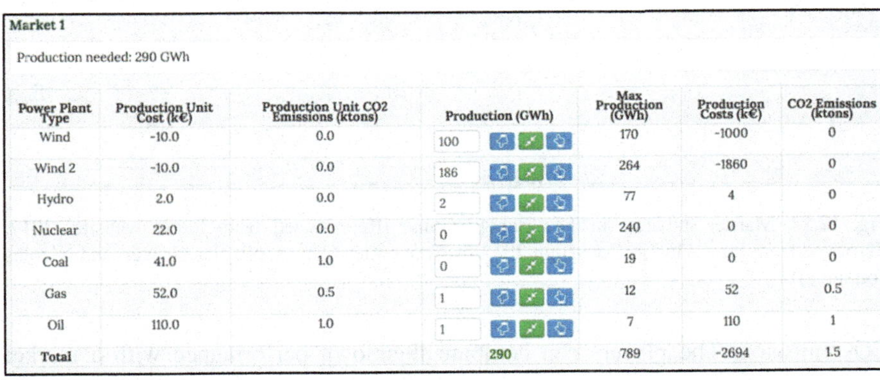

Market 1

Production needed: 290 GWh

Power Plant Type	Production Unit Cost (k€)	Production Unit CO2 Emissions (ktons)	Production (GWh)	Max Production (GWh)	Production Costs (k€)	CO2 Emissions (ktons)
Wind	-10.0	0.0	100	170	-1000	0
Wind 2	-10.0	0.0	186	264	-1860	0
Hydro	2.0	0.0	2	77	4	0
Nuclear	22.0	0.0	0	240	0	0
Coal	41.0	1.0	0	19	0	0
Gas	52.0	0.5	1	12	52	0.5
Oil	110.0	1.0	1	7	110	1
Total			290	789	-2694	1.5

Fig. 12.9 Electricity production planning in The Energy Game (Reproduced from lud.io website, 2017, Retrieved from https://lud.io Copyright 2017 by Economics Games, Nicolas Gruyer, and Nicolas Toublanc)

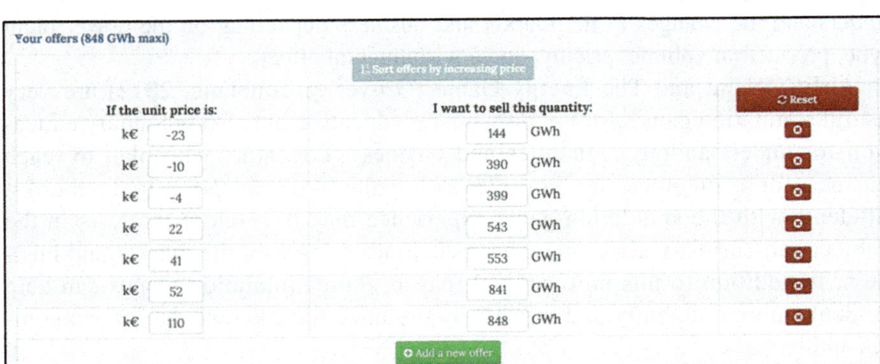

Your offers (848 GWh maxi)

1. Sort offers by increasing price

Reset

If the unit price is:	I want to sell this quantity:
k€ -23	144 GWh
k€ -10	390 GWh
k€ -4	399 GWh
k€ 22	543 GWh
k€ 41	553 GWh
k€ 52	841 GWh
k€ 110	848 GWh

Add a new offer

Fig. 12.10 Electricity pricing by sales quantity in The Energy Game (Reproduced from lud.io website, 2017 Retrieved from https://lud.io Copyright 2017 by Economics Games, Nicolas Gruyer, and Nicolas Toublanc)

	* Team 1 (1)	Robot Corp (2)
Sales	635 / 861 GWh	308 / 622 GWh
Revenue over the Round (excluding CO2 and exceptional)	k€47,625	k€23,100
Fixed Costs over the Round (excluding CO2 and exceptional)	k€33,580	k€15,098
Production Cost over the Round	-k€1,317	k€1,176
Profit over the Round (excluding CO2 and exceptional)	k€15,362	k€6,826
CO2 emissions over the round (ktons)	5.5	0

Fig. 12.11 Sales results in The Energy Game (Reproduced from lud.io website, 2017, Retrieved from https://lud.io Copyright 2017 by Economics Games, Nicolas Gruyer, and Nicolas Toublanc)

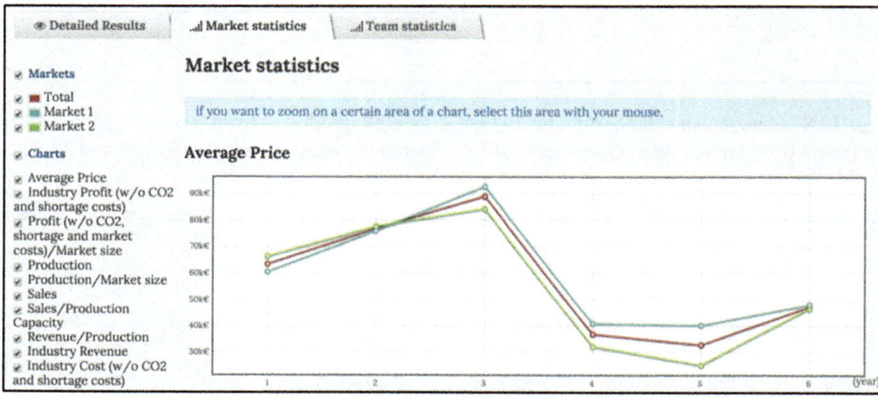

Fig. 12.12 Market statistics in The Energy Game (Reproduced from lud.io website, 2017, Retrieved from https://lud.io Copyright 2017 by Economics Games, Nicolas Gruyer, and Nicolas Toublanc)

CO_2 emission. The players can compare their own performance with a market competitor's.

After managing the electricity business for a few years in the game, the player can see a report showing detailed business results, market statistics, and team statistics. Figure 12.12 shows market statistics. With this statistics report, the player can understand the changes in the market and business depending on the power plant type, production volume, pricing, and environmental effect.

AirECONsim and The Energy Game (Gruyer & Toublanc, 2012) are very useful simulation games for not only higher education but also secondary education for understanding economics and business. Educators who plan to teach business or economics can consider using these games prior to textbooks. Students with the simulation game experience may have more interests in the subject and curiosity about the reasons behind changes in the market and business. In addition to this motivational reason, these simulation games can help students more efficiently and effectively organize their knowledge on economics and business.

12.4 Deloitte Leadership Academy

Deloitte Consulting established Deloitte Leadership Academy (DLA) for providing its employees with training programs. As one can imagine, most consultants have a packed schedule every day. This causes them to delay their learning. DLA tried to solve this problem with gamification.

DLA gamified its training programs with Badgeville (2016) game mechanics including badges, points, and leaderboards (Bodnar, 2014; Meister, 2013). Learners receive badges when they complete special missions. Also, if all members in a team successfully complete a specific mission within a limited time, they all can receive a special badge. As another game mechanics, micro leaderboards are also used. They show top ten rankers in each group and are updated each week.

With gamification, DLA implemented a system that provides immediate feedback on learning progress, scaffolding for right learning paths, and a means for motivation and engagement. As results, DLA could see dramatic improvements in course completion speed (50% faster), daily return rates (46.6% higher), and weekly retention rates (36.6% higher) (Bodnar, 2014).

From a viewpoint of the enterprise resource management, the gamification of DLA has contributed to the effective management of human resources with different expertise by easily locating and assigning optimal consultants for a specific project that requires subject-matter knowledge.

References

Badgeville. (2016). *Badgeville*. Available from https://badgeville.com/

Bodnar, Z. (2014). Using game mechanics to enhance leadership education. *Elearn, 2014*(2). doi:10.1145/2578511.2583703

Duolingo. (2011). *Duolingo*. Available from https://www.duolingo.com

Gruyer, N., & Toublanc, N. (2012). *Lud.io*. Available from https://lud.io

McGraw-Hill Education. (2012). *Practice series*. Available from https://www.mhpractice.com

Meister, J. (2013, January 2). *How Deloitte made learning a game*. Retrieved from https://hbr.org

Chapter 13
Gamify Your Instruction

Quest
Let's experience gamification cases introduced in the previous chapters.
Let's make gamified instruction.

13.1 Experience Gamification of Learning!

Originality is nothing but judicious imitation. The most original writers borrowed one from another – Voltaire, French writer and philosopher in the eighteenth century.

Many writers imitate other works as an exercise. They try to find and remember impressive expressions and styles from other works, mostly famous or highly reputed works. Unless they use the imitated part as their own, it is not a bad idea to imitate other works. For practice purposes, the imitation is a useful way to learn new or better writing styles and expressions.

Likewise, educators can imitate the gamification elements and methods from other gamification cases. The gamification cases introduced in this book can be useful resources for practice purposes. One important thing educators must remember is to experience the gamification cases as a learner as well as a teacher or administrator. Many gamification platforms or games provide tools that help educators observe students' behaviors but lack the means to understand the causes of their behavioral and emotional changes. Without direct experience of gamification or games as a learner or player, the understanding of students' behaviors and emotions can be very limited and superficial.

If an educator has no experience of gamification or games, playing a game can be an option to get familiar with gamification. The game does not need to be a serious game with specific educational purposes. "Clash of Clans (Supercell, 2012)" or "SimCity BuildIt" (Electronic Arts Inc., 2013) can be good choices to explore the game mechanics including point, level, avatar, narrative, reward, leaderboard, team

S. Kim et al., *Gamification in Learning and Education*, Advances in Game-Based Learning, DOI 10.1007/978-3-319-47283-6_13

play, virtual currency, virtual goods, and virtual market. With these games, the educator with limited understanding of gamification or games can see how each game mechanic works in the game and how a player can recognize and use it.

After exploring some gamification cases and games, each should be followed by a reflection of game mechanics. Some educators may focus on how the game mechanics can be effectively used for specific instruction. Some others may have more interest in finding an appropriate gamification platform or gamification case that can be applied to their whole program or organization. In either case, it might be meaningful to try to gamify instruction since an educator can learn lessons from the practical experience of designing gamification for education.

13.2 Gamify Your Own Instruction

Before gamifying your instruction, it may be helpful to review Chaps.7, 8, and 9. These chapters discuss students' perceptions of gamification, gamification frameworks, and gamification strategies.

Now, let's start to gamify your instruction. What should be the first step? The first step should be selecting the instruction that will be gamified. If it is the first time for you to gamify instruction, selecting an appropriate lesson is very important since some instruction is not easy to gamify due to its structure, content, or other characteristics. The following are characteristics of the types of instructions that make gamification difficult:

- Complexity of content: If the instruction is about complicated theories or too complex to easily understand, it is inappropriate as a first gamification attempt.
- Scope of instruction: The scope of instruction influences the complexity and difficulty of the gamification. If the scope is too large, there are more chances to have a problem in creating a story and designing mechanics.
- Number of students: There are various gamer types in gamified instruction. As the number of students increases, a gamification designer or educator needs to prepare more means and possible scenarios to meet various requirements.

Unless you have enough experience in gamification for educational purposes, it would be better to begin with a simple lesson with less complex content, shorter learning period, small scope, and small class size. In addition to these types of instruction characteristics, there are some other factors that make the gamification design process difficult:

- Number of mechanics: Each mechanic in the gamified instruction should work as a part of an organism, not a separated element. The mechanics should be connected to each other in order to make the gamification work effectively. Because of this reason, the number of mechanics should be carefully considered. If the number of mechanics for an instruction is five or more, it would be better to prioritize them and reduce the number.

- Level of technology: Using a realistic game graphic for instruction can help students become immersed in the learning experience. Designing gamification using advanced technologies requires a game designer or educator to handle more issues in different areas. For a first gamification, it would be a practical approach to use familiar and immediately available technologies and resources.

Although it is still possible to gamify instruction with many game mechanics or advanced technologies, it is not recommended to involve complex structures and unmanageable conditions. Having too many game mechanics is not the only issue of concern, but also challenging is the increase of the relationships among game mechanics and other elements in gamification. For example, when a problem occurs in gamification, the inclusion of more game mechanics makes the problem-solving process more difficult.

Some educators may consider using gamified instruction with immersive graphic designs to engage their students. However, unless the immersive graphic designs are embedded in a gamification platform that the educators plan to use, using advanced technologies can make gamification more difficult in terms of organizing a development team and maintenance of a gamified instructional program. Although there are no standard rules, the information in Table 13.1 can serve as a guide for selecting an instruction that can be a first gamification practice.

After selecting instruction for your first gamification effort, it would be a good idea to review instructional design models and theories with an emphasis on analyzing performance gaps, learners, and contexts. No matter what kind of interventions, including gamification, will be used for solving problems, it is significant to understand the goal, audience, and background. If you are not familiar with instructional design models and theories, you may find some useful information from the online resources in Table 13.2.

Table 13.1 Guidance for selecting a first gamified instruction

Category	Guidance
Content	Foundational and easy concepts
Scope	One lesson shorter than 40 min
Class size	About ten students
No. of mechanics	Three mechanics
Technology level	Technologies easy to use for both instructors and students

Table 13.2 Online resources on instructional design models and theories

Names	URLs
InstructionalDesign.Org	http://www.instructionaldesign.org
Big Dog & Little Dog's performance juxtaposition	http://www.nwlink.com/~donclark/hrd.html
Instructional design central	https://www.instructionaldesigncentral.com/instructionaldesignmodels
International Society for Educational Technology	http://educationaltechnology.net/category/frameworks-and-theories/

After the analysis phase, revisiting Chaps. 7 and 8 may remind you of what you should do for the following processes. You should find strategies for motivation and engagement in the course of designing gamified instruction. It is common that a novice gamification designer worries about the strategies since the designer is not sure if the strategies will work for the instruction. However, there will be a chance to evaluate and improve the strategies, usually through a pilot test. If the strategies are based on the results of the analysis phase, you may assume they will work. After accumulating practical knowledge on gamification, you can evaluate the strategies more quickly and effectively. Thus, it is a good approach to accept the fact that you are not a gamification expert yet.

After running your first gamified instructional program, there will be various kinds of feedback on the instruction. Some students may absentmindedly say that the instruction is interesting and motivates them. Some others may claim that the instruction makes them feel like a kid. You do not need to be disappointed with somewhat general or negative feedback from your students. You are just a level one player in terms of gamification in learning and education. What you need to do is to increase your experience points in the game, called gamification in learning and education.

References

Electronic Arts Inc. (2013). *SimCity BuildIt*. Available from https://www.ea.com

Supercell. (2012). *Clash of Clans*. Available from http://supercell.com

Index

S. Kim et al., *Gamification in Learning and Education*, Advances in Game-Based Learning, DOI 10.1007/978-3-319-47283-6

CPSIA information can be obtained
at www.ICGtesting.com
Printed in the USA
BVOW07*1413220917
495657BV00001B/1/P

9 783319 472829